Mark was born in 1963 in the bathroom of a suburban semi-detached house in Liverpool, where he grew up with his parents and brother, spending several years working in what he describes as 'dead-end jobs', before moving to London during the 1980s.

Mark loved the hectic lifestyle of London – a place where he met his beautiful wife, Lynne, and after their first son was born, Mark settled into life based around routine employed as a forklift driver until, somewhat ironically, a life-changing accident gave him the opportunity to pursue his passion in art, graduating with a BA hons degree at the University of East London in 2000. He has since sold artwork in conjunction with themed exhibitions focusing on contemporary issues such as animal welfare and global warming.

In recent years, Mark has concentrated on teaching, incorporating art into English lessons to help students with special needs gain nationally recognised qualifications. During the Covid pandemic, he returned to his old friend art and is now showcasing and selling work on media platforms such as Fine Art America and Art-Pal.

I dedicate this book to my lovely wife and soulmate Lynne. And to our dearest sons James and Christopher, our best friends and constant source of inspiration.

Mark Cawood

HEAVY RAINBOWS

AUSTIN MACAULEY PUBLISHERS™

LONDON • CAMBRIDGE • NEW YORK • SHARJAH

A CIP catalogue record for this title is available from the British Library.

ISBN 9781035838936 (Paperback)
ISBN 9781035838943 (Hardback)
ISBN 9781035838950 (ePub e-book)

www.austinmacauley.com

First Published 2024
Austin Macauley Publishers Ltd®
1 Canada Square
Canary Wharf
London
E14 5AA

I would like to thank *Sutton Community Academy* and especially Director Liz Barrett for her help, support and guidance during my time teaching there. And my lecturer Sheridan Brown, who, during my teacher training, taught me the importance of individual learning strategies for supporting students with special needs.

Aileen and Mike Mitchell, owners of *artgallery.co.uk*, who offered me the opportunity to exhibit my collection of *Distance* seascapes across the UK, paintings that focus on global warming and the potentially catastrophic consequences including rising sea levels and subsequent flooding.

Austin Macauley Publishers for giving me the opportunity to publish my autobiography and give members of the public the opportunity to read my unique and personal story, which I hope offers a sense of optimism and self-belief for anyone who has endured turbulent times.

Table of Contents

01 Art by Misadventure

I was just a few hours old when the most innovative band of all time recorded their debut album *Please Please Me* on the 13th February 1963, a prelude to what is now affectionately referred to as the *swinging sixties.* It was a time of hope and optimism, with an economy booming and no unemployment worries. There were new opportunities for everyone and for the first time, the average working-class family could afford their own car. Whether it be the economic fuel-saving Austin Mini, the gas-guzzling Ford Zephyr saloon or, for the more adventurous, the beautiful E-Type Jaguar sports car.

The affordable package holiday abroad was invented and Costa Blanca became the new Blackpool. The latest range of high fashion clothing and accessories were now accessible to millions with the introduction of mass produced polyester imitations.

Art and functionality began to work in harmony, with musicians singing about their newfound freedom involving sex, drugs and rock 'n' roll. And pop artist Andy Warhol created his now iconic screen-prints, satirising how everyone and everything is intrinsically involved with consumerism, from Marilyn Monroe to a simple can of mass produced soup.

Throughout the sixties and seventies our mum would take my brother and I on the bus every Sunday to visit our nan who lived in a large old terraced house in Toxteth, which had an outside toilet that everyone referred to as the *air raid shelter*.

When we arrived, the living room would usually be full of aunties and uncles conversing loudly with cousins, shouting and wrestling and when the excitement became too much, the obligatory fight would break out. Rather than compete with the television noise, nan often turned the sound down in an attempt to hear the multiple conversations that were being conducted simultaneously across the smoke-filled room.

On one particular occasion, with the television sound muted, I was distracted by sped up footage of four men, full of energy, jumping and running crazily around a large open field. I remember finding the footage very strange, though amusing and visually stimulating. The sight of grown-ups being utterly silly and not taking life so seriously was a breath of fresh air and something I'd never experienced before.

On reflection, I'm now aware this funny black and white film that had caught my attention as a child was actually footage from The Beatles art film *Hard Day's Night*.

As a young person I predominantly communicated visually rather than orally. I have no recollection of being read stories during my childhood and so accompanying pictures became my predominant source for understanding the content and narrative of a book.

During Christmas in 1969, I received a *Land of the Giants* annual and remember opening the first page of my new Christmas present. I couldn't understand any of the text so began scrutinising the accompanying colour illustration, an imposing silhouette of a tall giant appearing menacingly at the doorway. The image looked exciting and gave a teasing clue regarding the opening storyline, but I remember vividly my frustration at not being able to read the page and know exactly what the giant was doing in the hallway.

A year or so later, whilst at school, we were asked to draw a person so I drew this child with a massive big head and small thin body, the child's features were sad containing big sorrowful eyes. My teacher was hugely impressed and even appeared excited when showing my picture to fellow teachers. It was the first time I remember receiving such praise from a teacher and my picture was even framed and hung proudly in the corridor for everyone to see, which gave a huge boost to my self-confidence.

On reflection, I believe the teacher thought I'd captured the contemporary issue of children starving in Africa. Perhaps I'd seen images on the news and subconsciously relayed such information into the drawing, I'm not sure, but I was far too young to be conveying contemporary political issues through drawings.

However, the experience had taught me how drawing could have a powerful impact on adults, even sensible people such as teachers and was an attainable means to receive positive attention.

During my third year in junior school, aged around nine, my friend, Stephen, who remains a close friend today, had found an old keyring on the floor depicting a naked couple in a compromising position and asked me to copy the image onto paper for him. I felt complimented with being asked and enthusiastically accepted the challenge. During playtime, he handed me the keyring and I began making a copy in class, which I found far more interesting than the tedious work set out by my teacher, Mr Jones.

I remember being pleased with the development of my creative artwork and feeling rather self-satisfied as children opposite looked on in admiration whilst however, their gaze altered intermittently between my drawing and above my head, then suddenly and out of nowhere, a large hairy sun-burnt hand came into view and slowly yet deliberately picked up my erotic drawing.

There was a momentary silence within the classroom as Mr Jones digested the lurid adult content of my drawing. His facial expression grew visibly more intense, with eyes fixed sternly on the paper as the sweat on his forehead began to shine. He looked at me then back to the paper, you could have heard a pin drop until he whispered in a growling tone, "What is this?" by now I was frightened and merely shrugged my shoulders.

The silence was deafening until eventually he began to scream, as the shrieking continued I noticed his veins began to bulge out from his neck and the colour of his face turned an increasingly deeper purple.

Eventually, the class was allowed to leave for playtime, then the screaming and leg stamping recommenced. I don't recall Mr Jones' words, I was far too scared, though it was obvious he was disgusted at the erotic content of my artwork and not in the least interested how the work had been executed to a technically high standard.

This was another important lesson I'd learnt regarding the power of the image however, more importantly, the experience had taught me about rules and boundaries concerning the content of my drawings and what was considered acceptable and unacceptable or even offensive, regarding social etiquette and moral decency.

Aged ten I recall spending a lovely Sunday afternoon out with my mum, nan and younger cousin Christopher. We'd been walking for miles around Sefton Park in Toxteth, close to where my nan lived. It was a beautiful hot summer's day and we were given a lovely ice cream before fishing with our nets that were attached to long bamboo sticks that we'd purchased earlier. It was exciting catching tadpoles and newts from the lake before carefully placing them inside the jars nan had provided.

At the end of a thoroughly enjoyable yet tiring day, mum and I boarded the number seventy-three bus to take us home. I remember clearly, as the bus approached a well-known area called Penny Lane, I spoke to mum a couple of times and received no response. When I looked at her face, she appeared emotionless and expressionless.

Initially, I thought, *Oh no, what have I done wrong this time?* But she wasn't telling me off and that's what I found confusing. I tried to communicate a couple more times but mum appeared completely oblivious to my presence. I looked again and noticed her eyes were glossy, she looked traumatised, distraught, broken and remained in this state for the remainder of the journey and even after we got off the bus and for the rest of the evening, she remained silent and unresponsive.

This episode served as a dramatic shock introduction to mental health which, at the time, I was completely unprepared for and did not know what to do. Now, fifty years on, I'm aware my mum came from a closely knit family in Toxteth, near the centre of Liverpool where her sisters, brother and her beloved mum all lived.

After getting married, my parents bought their first home in Woolton, a suburban village about six miles out from where she'd lived all her life. Mum once told me how she initially didn't like Woolton because the area made her feel lonely and completely cut off from her family. I believe her feelings of isolation were compounded when dad, a Merchant Navy Sea Captain, spent months away at sea.

Around the same time, aged ten, whilst at primary school our teacher Mr Haycock assigned the class with a long-term project, the content of which was flexible and could be about anyone of our own choice, which introduced us to the concept of researching a subject independently and away from the traditional classroom environment.

Being interested in art, I chose Vincent Van Gogh and enjoyed the relevant freedom and responsibility involved with such an assignment, particularly as I was comfortable learning about an artist whose work I already admired. Research for the project taught me how Van Gogh had struggled with personal mental health and had lived somewhat awkwardly within contemporary western society, information that helped me understand the motive behind his early paintings of hard-working peasants.

Regrettably, I threw my Van Gogh project away however, following a recent house move, I found a large battered cardboard box stored in our loft which contained a collection of old artwork drawn with my left hand during my schooldays and amongst one of the oldest was a portrait of Vincent Van Gogh, that I'd drawn for my project.

By the time I'd reached eleven, it was obvious my strongest subject in the classroom was art and consequently I became interested in developing my ability. I started looking around people's rooms to see what I could draw or paint.

During the summer holidays in 1974 we were staying at my gran's home in Yorkshire, I asked whether I could paint one of her poppies that were on display in a delicate looking ceramic vase, my request was granted and I enthusiastically lifted the petite red flower from the vase, to protests from dad who was immediately overruled by gran, as I gently rested my new delicate subject on the coffee table.

I was delighted with the completed painting, which I felt possessed a professional quality, as it hadn't obviously been painted by a child and proudly showed my work to gran, who responded, "That's champion Mark." During the following months, I painted several versions and even painted a couple inside birthday cards that I sent to friends.

By the age of twelve, I was proactively taking steps to improve my technical drawing and painting skills and bought a tutorial book containing a variety of exercises on how to draw people's faces accurately, which helped enormously. My motivation was to master the ability of creating realistic colour portraits and I started experimenting with various paints, such as watercolours, gouache and oils.

During this period I ended up feeling most comfortable with water-based poster paints and soon learnt the basic combination of colours required to create subtle flesh tones in relation to light and shade using red, yellow, white and a small amount of blue for darker shades, which I incorporated into my portraits.

Aged thirteen, I often drew our lovely pet dog *Smudge* who served as a great subject, particularly whilst asleep.

The choice of medium is interesting, a felt-tip pen which left no room for error as mistakes would be impossible to erase.

Aged fourteen, I'd become disenchanted with school and had lost all motivation, which resulted in truancy and repeatedly getting into trouble, receiving the cane on several occasions for fighting or smoking.

Mr Breeze was my year head who inflicted the cane and always said prior to the act, "This is going to hurt me far more than it's going to hurt you." A phrase which puzzled me greatly, as I couldn't understand why someone would carry out such an act of violence if it hurt them so much.

Luckily during this period, I attended a youth club which had easy-going supportive members of staff and a close-knit group of friends who were also suffering with adolescent related problems, frequently discussed during lazy summer days spent in the park whilst sharing a smoke. Other popular subjects included music, girlfriends and the venue for our next party.

I'd started listening to progressive rock bands such as *ELP* (Emerson, Lake and Palmer), *Pink Floyd* and *Yes*. I had ELP's album *Pictures at an Exhibition*, the cover of which contains a collection of blank picture frames that I thought could be enhanced if one of them were filled in with an appropriate painting.

The progressive rock album contains abstract content and so I created a relevant painting that plays around with realism and scale, conveying a large spiritual figure in the sky looking down on three tiny figures that represent Emerson, Lake and Palmer.

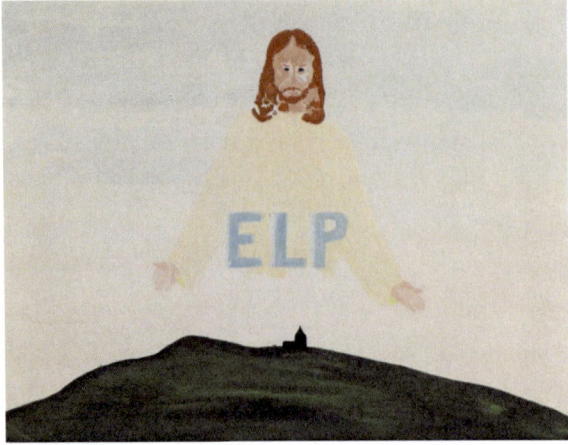

Resulting in my first attempt at creating a Surreal painting, which happens to be dated precisely on the back, stating it was completed on the 7 July 1977.

Around this period in my life, my friend Stephen and I would share a packet of fags and often sat on the steps for a smoke in the grounds of our local church. It was St Peter's in Liverpool where teenagers John Lennon and Paul McCartney first met at a summer fair about twenty years earlier.

On one occasion the vicar greeted us at the steps, I was anticipating being ordered to make ourselves scarce, on the contrary, the vicar was very pleasant, turned a blind eye as we hastily stubbed out our cigarettes and asked politely if we'd be interested in earning some money. Our eyes lit up and the vicar had our undivided attention.

The next thing I remember, Stephen and I were inside the church steeple holding onto thick decorative ropes attached to several large church bells situated high up in the steeple. The vicar gave clear and concise instructions on the art of bell ringing before taking a bow and stepping back with a reassuring smile.

I volunteered to ring the bells first. The rope was heavy and needed a strong tug, nothing happened so I gave a second more robust tug then, suddenly, as I heard the loud sound of a church bell, I was catapulted rapidly into the air at a frightening speed high up into the steeple. I held tight on to the rope as if my life depended on it, as the vicar and Stephen rapidly diminished in size, their heads looking up at my rapid ascendance. Finally, I let go and crashed unceremoniously onto the floor in a bedraggled heap.

It had been a frightening experience and, on reflection, a somewhat unforgettable crash-course in learning the principles of perspective and vanishing points. I think my near death experience had deterred Stephen a little and he refused to pull the rope hard enough to get the bells to ring. We thanked the vicar for offering us a bell ringing job opportunity but cordially and rather sheepishly, declined before saying our goodbyes.

Aged fourteen to sixteen, I studied for my art O'level with teacher Mr Chambers. Lessons involved learning about perspective, vanishing points and shading, which I found thoroughly interesting and served to improve the technical accuracy of my drawing skills. At home, I would utilise such knowledge to create accurate drawings of subjects I found interesting at the time, such as classic vehicles.

Each week we were given a still-life drawing exercise to complete at home in our sketchbooks, such as a cup & saucer or an old shoe.

At the beginning of each lesson, my friend Ian and I would compare our still-life drawings and attempt to predict what score, out of ten, our work would receive from Mr Chambers. We were competitive and consequently motivated to do a good drawing in order to beat each other's score. I have fond memories of this period at school, particularly as I usually achieved the higher score.

My art O'level exam was due the day after a week's holiday in Spain with my parents. We arrived home late in the evening and after a quick sandwich, I hurriedly sketched out my preparation drawings that had to be handed in during the practical exam the following morning. I woke up excited rather than feeling jet-lagged, this was going to be my last day at school and all I had to do was draw a picture before leaving, for good!

On entering the classroom I saw what we were required to draw for the practical, a group of plants were displayed in the centre of each table. *Great,* I thought to myself, *if only all exams could be this easy.*

Several weeks later my friend Ian called to inquire what grade I'd received, it transpired we'd both been awarded a grade 'B', to which I was very pleased. Ian, in contrast, was deeply upset because he'd spent months preparing and planning his preparation drawings. Ian was a great friend and played a positive influence on me during those testing times as a teenager in secondary school and he went on to become a great art teacher in Liverpool. Unfortunately, we eventually lost touch, probably due to us both moving homes several times and living in different areas.

At sixteen I left school to work for Greenberg's Ltd, a Merchant Navy outfitter, which I enjoyed but left to join the Merchant Navy. However, after just one day at the training base, I decided the military orientation of the training programme wasn't for me and I left the following day, which to this day I regret. Travelling the seven seas would have been a wonderful adventure and my favourite form of travel is by ship, particularly in stormy weather.

After leaving school, my drawing continued, usually consisting of doodles whilst relaxing with friends. I often found myself sketching someone's portrait and if it was any good I'd give the impromptu image to my sitter, otherwise it would be thrown in the bin.

I worked in a warehouse for WH Smith's for the next six years, which I hated with a passion, before moving to Peckham in East London aged twenty-three. There I held several jobs, including working for *Reader's Digest,* where I met Lynne at the Christmas Party in December 1986. We fell in love and became parents in April 1988 with our lovely son,

James. Moved to Essex where I got a job working as a forklift driver with the electrical company Thorn EMI.

There was always plenty of overtime and the money was good. I enjoyed the company of my colleagues, which involved plenty of banter and small talk regarding our favourite football teams and whether or not they'd performed well during a game the previous night. When there wasn't much work to be done, we'd pass the time by rolling up several sheets of paper wrapped in brown tape and have our own football match.

In the summer of 1989, Lynne, James and I had a fantastic week's holiday in a work colleagues' caravan in Clacton-on-Sea.

On the first day we were browsing in the caravan park's souvenir shop and noticed a lovely ceramic plate with a relief image of two cats hugging. At six pounds, we thought it was too expensive and decided to look for something else. Just before we were due to catch our train home, we still hadn't bought a souvenir to remember our first family holiday and so returned to the caravan shop, realising we just about had enough money to buy the ceramic plate which is now proudly displayed in our hallway.

Seven months later, I suffered a catastrophic life-changing motorcycle accident whilst on the way to work early in the morning of 7 March 1990, aged twenty-seven.

02 My Big Break

I awoke feeling drowsy from what seemed like a long and deep sleep, my head felt heavy and groggy. I could hear the background noises of busy people talking and shouting. I realised family members, including Lynne, our son James and my mum and dad, were all standing around my bed. So I knew immediately that something strange was happening. A female voice told me I'd been in an accident on my motorcycle and had broken my arm, I don't remember much after this initial introduction to my new life and, feeling utterly exhausted, fell back to sleep.

Oldchurch Hospital in Essex would be my new home for the next few months. I'd punctured my left lung, my left leg was in plaster due to a shattered kneecap and, after a couple of weeks, it became apparent I'd permanently paralysed my dominant left arm.

There were two other long-term patients in my ward and we became close over time. Mick was a confident, outgoing character who told rather colourful stories about his exploits as a pilot and regularly had beer smuggled in by his girlfriend, which fellow patients found very amusing.

Tom, another long-term patient, had broken his ankle as a result of jumping from the top of a shopping mall escalator whilst high on drugs. We had plenty of time on our hands and often talked about our interests, family, jobs, hobbies. And our aspirations, hopes and concerns for the future. My partner Lynne and our two-year-old son James, who I don't think was old enough to fully understand what had happened, visited every day which I cherished.

When Mick's girlfriend was due to visit, Tom and I kept a lookout for the nurses and especially the matron, an uncompromising person who prohibited all alcohol from her ward, whilst packs of beer cans were slipped swiftly beneath Mick's bed. The event served as a great antidote to the monotony of life in a hospital ward and developed into a rather exciting game of cat and mouse.

My first steps concerning recovery were made out of necessity, I had been left-handed prior to the accident and consequently had to learn basic everyday tasks involving learning to dress, brush my teeth, shave and go to the toilet using my right hand. Initially, I grew a beard after several failed attempts at shaving, which merely highlighted the potential danger of using a sharp razor blade.

One new patient on our ward spent most of his time creating large bright cartoons of famous Disney characters that were accurately drawn and coloured in beautifully. It was a talking point and both patients and nurses were impressed. When someone asked whether he'd ever considered doing it for a living, I distinctly remember thinking to myself that, whatever I do for a living when I finally leave the hospital, it most certainly will NOT involve drawing pictures.

On one occasion the matron summoned me to a room where I spent several hours with an Occupational Therapist, to receive guidance and encouragement on mastering tasks with my right hand, such as tying a shoelace and cracking an egg into a frying pan, which I achieved successfully and subsequently felt a million dollars.

The day got even better when I returned to the ward, greeted by Mick and his cheesy big smile, who'd just received a visit and a new batch of alcohol from his girlfriend. On hearing how well I'd done with the Occupational Therapist, he awarded me with a four pack of lager—and it wasn't long before we were both wearing cheesy big smiles.

After three and a half months and several operations I was finally discharged, it was time to go home and face the real world in our third-floor flat in Barking, Essex. I had been offered an ambulance to take me home but Lynne's parents kindly offered to give me a lift. I was in the rear seat with Lynne sitting next to me and her parents were in the front, her dad John was driving and every time we went over the slightest bump, my shoulder hurt intensely, which brought home the extent of my frail condition.

The following morning, I remember waking up in the flat and, for the first time since my accident, feeling utterly incapacitated, disabled and scared, scared of what the future may hold and how I would support my family. It was a dreadful lonely feeling with the safety of my hospital ward and the bubble it provided, now gone. It was time to face reality, whether I was ready or not.

A representative from my employers, Thorn EMI, visited our home to advise that after lengthy discussions between management, union representatives and personnel, it had been decided that someone with a paralysed arm would not be able to operate a forklift truck safely and so, with deep regret, my employment had been terminated and when my holiday pay expired, I'd automatically be transferred onto disability benefit. The Thorn EMI representative had brought a bag of sweets for our son James, I assume, to soften the bad news.

Four months after my accident, on a hot and humid evening at Upney Hospital in Essex on the 6 July 1990, Lynne gave birth to our lovely son Christopher, which on reflection had served as a positive distraction during my recovery process. Lynne and our two sons were marvellous and I felt deeply humbled how they appeared to accept my disability as merely being a fact of life. Though I couldn't help feeling incredibly guilty and that I'd let everyone down.

During the following months I'd become interested in a television cookery series presented by chef Kieth Floyd and I particularly liked the way he'd pour excessive amounts of alcohol into his pots and pans when cooking, before taking a mischievous swig for himself and smiling at the camera. It was time to take up a hobby and cooking was something Lynne and I could do together.

We created several lovely dishes, including stews, a variety of curry dishes and a splendid coq-au-vin. After investing in a quality wok and a couple of books, our culinary skills developed to more adventurous dishes, including stir-fries using a base of beansprouts, egg noodles, oyster sauce and vegetables served semi-raw.

One Saturday evening, after watching an episode of Keith Floyd, I was in the mood to create my own culinary masterpiece. The wok was hot, peppers, onions and prawns were added in a rather cavalier fashion, I splashed in a generous helping of brandy and suddenly whoosh! A bright flash enveloped my face, burning off the hair from my eyebrows which unfortunately have never grown back and to this day I have a constant expression of surprise across my face.

I joined the Essex Gliding Club where I met Gerry, a Black Cab Taxi Driver who loved a chat, had an easy-going personality and was a very kind soul. Every Wednesday morning I'd catch the train to Upminster in Essex where Gerry lived and he'd drive us both onto North Weald Aerodrome, where we'd fly a circuit around the airfield. He became a good friend and gave me an old clunky typewriter, which, little did I know at the time, would become an essential piece of equipment for my future academic escapades.

During this time, I took driving lessons in a little red Rover Metro and passed my test first time on the date of our youngest son's second birthday. I felt a great sense of achievement, having finally earned a degree of independence as well as hope that things were slowly but steadily getting better. Now was the time to seriously consider what I was going to do for a living.

My previous employer had terminated my job as a forklift driver due to having a paralysed arm, so my old profession was out of the question. I remember being in bed late one evening when I began thinking of potential possibilities for a future career. I thought about taxi driving and driving a van, but both occupations involved loading and unloading, which would be a problem.

What about working in an office? I thought before doubts crept in, I would struggle taking messages whilst holding the phone. I'd almost fallen asleep when I thought—*If I follow closely and meticulously those basic principles learnt at school during art lessons involving perspective, vanishing points and light, it might, just might be possible to complete a basic still-life composition using a good quality pencil, paper and, of course, a good rubber, for there would surely be mistakes.*

The next day, I woke up full of energy and feeling quite excited at the prospect of my new challenge. Lynne and I went shopping at the local mall where WH Smith sold stationery equipment. I remember choosing my resources carefully, which included several pencils, good quality cartridge paper, a pencil sharpener and, of course, a decent rubber.

I looked at my old sketchbook containing O'level coursework and decided to replicate the *cup and saucer* drawing, taken from a homework exercise sixteen years earlier. My preparation was thorough, requiring two small tables, one for the cup and saucer to be placed and one where I would sit with my drawing book and equipment carefully laid out, including pencils, rubber and sharpener.

My approach was slow and tentative, the HB pencil lines were applied lightly in order to rub out mistakes easily and I remained very conscious of abiding to the laws of perspective and to be sure the composition filled the page, as instructed by my art teacher, Mr Chambers, all those years ago.

After about two hours of intense concentration, 13 March 1994, I had successfully completed my very first drawing using my right hand.

Created with the help of my pencil sharpener, necessary to maintain a sharp point for detailed work and my dependable right-hand man, the rubber, which had been a lifesaver when the inevitable mistakes were made.

I was euphoric, ecstatic and over the moon, as if being reunited with a long-lost friend and was under no illusions just how ground-breaking my drawing exercise had been—the world was now my oyster!

The next few weeks consisted of further still-life exercises, including a pair of slippers, stack of books, daffodils in a vase and an old rusty padlock, which were used to capture different textures and perfect my drawing skills. An egg and spoon involved the enjoyable experience of capturing light reflecting from the metallic piece of cutlery.

It wasn't long before I began looking at art courses commencing later in the year. I made an impromptu visit to Barking College to enquire whether they delivered courses suitable for myself, i.e. someone who's been out of education for the past fifteen years. Their response was positive and encouraging and they appeared to have plenty of time to discuss and answer all of my concerns and queries.

The head art lecturer even came into the office, acknowledged I had good motivation and advised if my drawings were of a reasonable standard then, as a mature student, I could apply for an interview to enrol onto their two year full-time *Advanced Course in Art & Design.* We shook hands and a future date was arranged for me to take a tour with a lecturer.

The course leader, Jackie Galise, showed me around classrooms where students' artwork could be viewed hanging on the walls. I was impressed but immediately realised the diversity of the work, including fabrics, posters and sculptures. It became evident there remained a huge gulf between my quaint little pencil drawings and the *advanced* students' splendid and diverse artwork.

A few days later, I'd acquired a handful of chalk pastels, given generously by a sales assistant at my local art shop. I'd previously never used pastels before but felt it necessary to produce something more colourful and adventurers than my rather safe looking pencil drawings for my forthcoming interview.

My initial attempt at using pastels involved a portrait from the cover of one of Lynne's magazines. I remember how working with colour pastels were completely different from the monochrome pencil I'd become accustomed to and how soft, crumbly and unpredictable they were.

I found the texture of pastels similar to painting rather than drawing and, being completely unfamiliar with the medium, felt like I was entering unknown waters. Applying pastels to paper involves smudging rather than drawing and it soon became apparent that more detailed control could be achieved using thin edges of the pastel and faint shades were achieved using dry pieces of tissue (or earbuds) to reduce the pigments intensity.

My objective was to master control of chalk pastels competently enough to recreate an accurate representation of a portrait and, at this time, had no interest in creating anything stylised or abstract. To complete my portfolio for my interview at Barking College, I created several more colourful pastel paintings, including several developed from photographs of my two young sons.

I was interviewed by Jackie, the course leader, in an empty classroom where I proudly showed off my portfolio with the new colourful additions. On viewing my pastel paintings I was surprised with her reaction, which involved smiling prior to asking the age of my sons. "Four and six," I replied somewhat confused, as I'd anticipated my interview to involve technical questions such as inquiring how I'd acquired contrast, highlights or something similar regarding my work, rather than questions about my kids.

I was very motivated and keen to make a good impression during the interview, whereas Jackie's approach was far more laid back.

Anyway, she made me feel at ease and I liked her easy-going attitude. She told me there and then that I'd been accepted onto the course, commencing September. Jackie informed me a self-portrait would be required, as with all the students, for a presentation on the first day of the course, she then offered some technical information including dates, fees and where and when to report on the first day. I couldn't hide my delight, my smile must have stretched from ear to ear, we shook hands and said goodbye.

I returned home very excited and couldn't stop talking to Lynne about my new venture. I was deeply humbled with being accepted directly onto an *advanced* course. The other students would surely be intelligent, capable and well-motivated creators and it would be important to hold my own, at least compete, during this two-year full-time course.

03 Lessons

The first day consisted of group bonding activities to help break the ice between fellow students. Our class consisted of twenty-six students mainly aged between eighteen and twenty-five and two mature students, Yousaf and myself, both in our early thirties.

It was time to produce our self-portraits, I was looking forward to this part of the day as it would be an opportunity to gauge the standard of work amongst my fellow students. Each of us had to show our work to the class and give a brief description of how they had been created, including the medium used and how long the portrait took. Some were good, however I was surprised how several appeared to have been rushed, that or they couldn't do portraits.

The course was full-time, intense and included a variety of subjects that required lots of revision and homework. After several weeks, I'd identified my favourite subjects as *Drawing & Painting, Media Exploration* and *History of Art. Information Technology* was by far my weakest subject where, during lessons, I learnt to ask for help from colleagues in order to complete the work.

Each and every project in all subjects required a written action plan and evaluation which I considered to be a complete waste of time and a somewhat unnecessary distraction to creating art, to which I bitterly resented doing. However, with time, I became aware that research could be interesting, offering knowledge and a deeper understanding of the subject involved.

During *History of Art* lessons we had a great lecturer, I was impressed with his in-depth subject knowledge, laid back delivery and a refusal to suffer fools, several of whom served as fodder to his sharp wit and dry sense of humour. I enjoyed his classes, where I developed a greater understanding of art movements from the past and relevant cultures, such as the *Surrealists*, their interest in dreams and how they evolved from the anarchic *Dada* movement.

We were introduced to *Impressionism*, a radical art movement formed in Paris during the eighteen-sixties, largely in response to the invention of photography, which had taken over the world of visual representation.

Now artists had to create a new alternative way of seeing. *Impressionists* revolutionised preconceived views of traditional art by creating quick loosely painted work that celebrated rather than hid brush strokes, which I found thoroughly enlightening and served to enrich my knowledge and understanding of alternative techniques such as impasto painting, which became a useful additional string to my bow for my own work.

We were introduced to the concept of *narrative art* and studied examples of relevant work by Titian, Rubens, Max Beckman and Picasso, amongst others. I chose to do a project on the great Vincent Van Gogh, covering his powerful paintings of peasants and farm workers whose plight he cared for deeply (according to contemporary letters written to friends and family). His later work incorporated bright vivid colouring such as the sunflowers and starry night paintings.

He spent the latter part of his life in a mental asylum where a supportive doctor and staff gave him all the resources necessary to continue with his painting where, arguably, he produced his most prolific work.

Van Gogh's style of work, containing an impromptu immediacy to create vivid imagery using heavy brushwork, is obviously influenced by the *Impressionists,* developed largely during his time in France though he's often referred to as a *Post Impressionist* and his incorporation of black linear work within many of his paintings is a characteristic difference to that of Impressionism.

The course involved several day trips to London, where there are plenty of galleries and museums full of beautiful paintings, sculptures and historic artefacts from a wealth of different cultures and periods. On one occasion, during a visit to *The Tate Modern* in Westminster, I'd just completed a rough sketch of a Titian masterpiece, *Bacchus and Ariadne* (1522–1523) just in time for our lunch break.

I returned to my car where I had a sandwich waiting in the glove compartment, only to find the front wheel had been clamped! I immediately became quite incensed, being fully aware I'd paid the parking fare in the adjacent metre. I ran back inside the gallery to inform fellow students what had happened. My colleague Yousaf smiled and immediately evoked a calming effect as he offered me his mobile phone, a rare luxury back in 1995 and invited me to phone Westminster Council concerning their dreadful mistake.

I was trying desperately to maintain composure despite my voice steadily growing louder as I walked through the quiet rooms within the grand *Tate Modern*: "Why have you clamped my car, when there's a valid ticket clearly visible in the front window?"

I entered another room where it was quiet apart from a softly spoken tour guide, she was describing historic details to her attentive party about an old oil painting hanging on the wall. The person I was speaking to kept insisting on payment before the clamp could be removed. I protested: "You have no right to clamp my car as I've paid the bloody parking fare."

The tour guide and her party tried to ignore the interruption but several turned to see where the commotion was coming from. I continued louder: "This is totally unacceptable and I demand you release my car!"

By now I was walking faster and virtually shouting and had become quite desperate: "How the hell am I going to get home?!"

Eventually, the person on the phone, from Westminster Council, suggested a payment of £30, as opposed to the £60 initially demanded, would be acceptable for the clamp to be removed.

When the Parking Officer turned up to release the clamp she told me they'd been fully aware I had made a genuine mistake prior to clamping my car, declaring with a smile, "We knew you'd put money in the wrong meter but rules are rules." I've never forgiven Westminster Council ever since.

From the twenty-six students who'd started the course, quite a few had failed to complete the gruelling two years. I was lucky enough to be awarded a distinction for my effort and three of us were accepted a place at university. The course had taught me a great deal in preparation for university. Academically, I'd developed a greater understanding of the importance of teamwork, research and planning and on a practical level, I'd been introduced to a wide variety of media, techniques and skills, some of which I use to this day.

I attended the *University of East London* in October 1996, initially studying *Illustration* on a part time basis. When I commenced my second year as a full-time student, the *Illustration* course had been scrapped and changed to *Graphic Fine Art*. Some students struggled with such a dramatic change and had constant trouble trying to adapt to fine art criteria.

Looking back, my favourite subject at university was *History of Art,* which involved learning about different genres, movements and cultures, a constant source of relevant information and is always very rewarding.

I was impressed with the subject knowledge and professionalism of my lecturer, Biddy Pepper. She would stretch and challenge her students and on several occasions we were required to prepare and deliver a presentation to our peers, which enriched our knowledge and enhanced our understanding of the subject concerned and she improved student confidence by giving us the experience of talking and interacting publicly.

One assignment required a slide presentation on *Cubism* that would be followed by a *question-and-answer* session between students afterwards. *Cubism* is a semi-abstract style of art created by Pablo Picasso and Andre Braque early in the twentieth century. The paintings portray an image from multiple vantage points and there's an emphasis on geometric angles and two-dimensional shapes, often used with a fairly neutral palette.

I chose Pablo Picasso's 1937 anti-war Cubist masterpiece *Guernica*, that illustrates an aerial bombing orchestrated by fascists during the Spanish Civil War. The large monochrome painting portrays a dying horse, screaming women, a dead baby and a dismembered soldier in a style accessible to the public.

Many art critics have described the work as the most moving and powerful anti-war painting in history. The painting was displayed to the public in France throughout the civil war, then exhibited in the USA during the Second World War before travelling around the world for the following twenty years.

Following my slide presentation, a student asked why Picasso would portray such a violent event using *childlike* images. I responded, "I believe Picasso used a semi-abstract Cubist style of painting to portray the horrific massacre of innocent women and children in order to permit global exposure of such an atrocious act of genocide."

I paused and realised I had the undivided attention of students and lecturer and so continued, "If Picasso had painted the event using realistic images of dismembered soldiers and dead babies, it is doubtful galleries and newspapers would have been allowed to show or publicise such a painting."

The subject had raised quite an intensive and emotionally charged debate and successfully highlighted the potential power of the image, particularly in the context of truth versus propaganda.

During my second year at university, I created a few Cubist-inspired renditions of Picasso's pioneering way of seeing.

And spent many hours experimenting in the print room with a variety of media, including screen-printing and steel or aluminium etchings. I concentrated on portraiture and made several steel plate etchings depicting friends and family, including my old school friend Stephen and his wife Ruth.

The process involves drawing or photographing your desired image onto a steel plate, which is then placed into a solution of acid, longer periods burn deeper into the plate and create bolder marks during the printing stage. The outcome of your print also depends on the amount of ink applied, more detailed effects such as shading can be obtained using chalk or tissues to rub off a limited amount of ink from specific areas to create the effect of light, shade and form.

Finally, heavy duty printing paper is put through a press to produce an individual print that must be left overnight to dry.

The Stephen & Ruth designs were developed from a series of photographs I'd taken, from which I chose the three most suitable for converting into steel etchings, i.e. each composition had to be simple and well defined and incorporate strong contrast. Stephen and Ruth chose their favourite print *(image 2)* and presently have it proudly on display in the living room of their home—a narrow boat on the beautiful Norfolk Broads.

Practical tuition was largely taught by lecturers, Eric and Martin, who advocated a post-modern course program which was fine by me as I naturally enjoyed experimenting with different media.

For the past two years, I'd experimented with screen-printing, lino printing, etchings, sculptures and collages. I'd played around with the conjunction of text and image, particularly with my screen-prints and digital imagery and felt confident my work would be viewed favourably by Eric and Martin.

In preparation for my final year's work and final year's exhibition, I would be focusing on contemporary social issues involving agriculture and how its economy affects animal welfare. My work would be illustrative rather than abstract and form a close relationship with reality.

However, by the time I'd reached my final year, the lecturer's obsession with experimentation and apparent contempt for narrative art was becoming problematic. Being a student, I rebelled and acquired a box of traditional oil paints, which I found a delight to work with and gave me an additional sense of satisfaction, aware the medium was not associated, academically, with experimentation.

During this period I watched Chris Olifi win the 1998 *Turner Prize* on television and remember being impressed with his collection of paintings including *No Woman No Cry,* a portrait of Doreen Lawrence, who campaigned relentlessly for an inquiry into the failed murder investigation of her teenage son, Stephen Lawrence, who was murdered during an unprovoked violent racist attack in 1993.

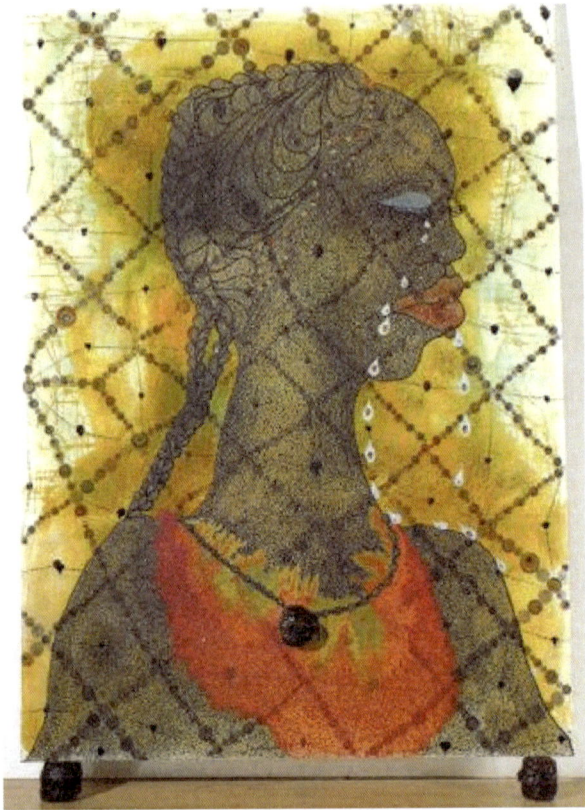

Eventually, Doreen was successful in her bid for an inquiry which concluded investigating officers had acted "incompetently—repeatedly lost evidence—[and]—the police had become institutionally racist." The painting was purchased by the *Tate Gallery* in 1999.

Materials used to create *No Woman No Cry* include acrylic and oil paint, polyester resin, elephant dung and various other stuff. Depicting a portrait of Doreen Lawrence with braided hair and crying, with each tear consisting of an image of her son Stephen. The large painting (96 inches high by 72 inches wide) is supported by two varnished lumps of dried elephant dung and a third lump forming part of Doreen's necklace.

I was inspired by the uncompromising political content of Chris Olifi's work and his outlook, "There are no rules and even the ones you set for yourself can be temporary." He influenced the direction of my work then, at university and still does to this day.

Tension between myself and the lecturers grew more intense regarding my insistence with illustrating contemporary issues relating to social issues such as animal welfare, in contrast to their promotion of a somewhat airy-fairy vacuous *post-modern* art which I felt had nothing to say. On reflection, perhaps it was simply a matter of there being no chemistry between myself and the lecturers.

In preparation for my final year's exhibition, I produced a large oil painting on wood entitled *Cow in Hand* and was particularly pleased with how it obviously compromised the course ethos of narrative abstinence. Initial plans for the painting consisted of a stylised horse being held in the hand, which I later changed for a more realistic looking cow.

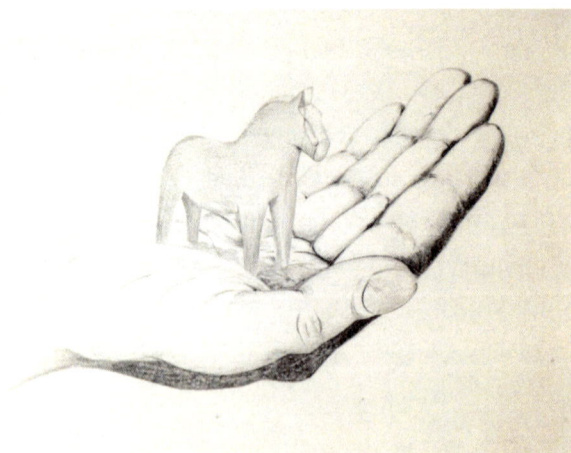

In addition to the *Cow in Hand* painting, my exhibition consisted of an installation with human faces made from raw chicken served with fine cutlery and quality ceramic plates on a large dining table complete with candles, tablecloth and matching serviettes. There were glasses and a customised bottle of red wine with a label stating it had been made with genetically modified grapes, which was a point of contention at the time.

Several weeks prior to our *Third Year Exhibition,* fellow student Matthew had created several large and technically impressive figure paintings which he showed me with enthusiasm and pride, declaring they were for the final exhibition, I congratulated him and offered an uplifting appraisal of his gifted ability.

I was, therefore, surprised to see his impressive set of figurative paintings conspicuously absent from his exhibition display stand, which were replaced with four pink helium balloons each floating from his stand on a few feet of string, where I noticed Matthew standing alongside looking visibly uncomfortable. I asked him what had happened to his beautiful figure paintings, to which he replied the lecturers had told him they were not suitable for the exhibition and had suggested "balloons" instead.

I couldn't help wondering whether Eric and Martin were amusing themselves at the expense of younger and perhaps more impressionable students.

Our exhibitions were set up and all our work handed in. Now, it was time for the end-of-year party. I enjoyed talking to family members of students I'd got to know well over the years during our time at university. The room was dark with flashing coloured lights, loud music playing, plenty of alcohol on the tables, students laughing, singing, dancing, some deep in conversation with lecturers, others pulling strained faces, apparently having trouble hearing the conversation.

The lights were low and Peter Gabriel's *Sledgehammer* was playing high, I'd exchanged a few pleasantries with a couple of lecturers before lighting up a spliff, nobody said anything and probably didn't notice in the dark crowded room, though I didn't much care. It was ten to ten and my taxi would be arriving at the car park soon. I stood up and immediately felt light-headed whilst walking slowly yet deliberately to the exit door.

The outside air was warm, still and fresh, it felt sublime. I felt relaxed, calm and happy. The taxi arrived, "Dagenham, mate?" the driver asked.

"Yep," I replied, climbed in and closed the door before we drove slowly out of the university car park. I felt a great sense of relief and slumped back into the chair. *No regrets—don't look back.*

I received a 2/1 BA Honours Degree in *Graphic Fine Art* in the summer of 2,000. After six long years studying as a mature student, I was keen to get out of education and felt excited at the prospect of creating new work for exhibitions and sales.

04 Food for Thought

After university, it felt a little strange having no project, assignment or essay to complete. However, there were a million things I wanted to do and so my newfound freedom was a welcome blessing.

My brother Malcolm is a web designer and offered to build a website for me to promote my artwork. We agreed to focus on the theme of *animal welfare* as I'd already been creating relevant work in preparation for exhibition proposals.

We worked hard on the venture for several months during 2001, which eventually developed into the *Food for Thought* project, incorporating a unique and alternative view of landscape artwork set within an agricultural theme to highlight how, in the name of 'good economic practise', factory farmed animals were being mistreated.

I created hundreds of high resolution jpeg images, designed especially for the *Food for Thought* project and after about nine very busy months Malcolm presented me with a highly sophisticated, professional looking site, domain name *Sputnik-Art* (named after my beautiful ginger cat), complete with clearly defined categories and links. I had been under the impression we were embarking on a joint crusade to raise concerns and perhaps even resolve injustices such as the barbaric treatment of farm animals by uniting our strengths, skills and knowledge.

However, it soon became apparent Malcolm's primary interest was to create an impressively designed website rather than get involved with contemporary social issues that I was highlighting through my art and, unfortunately, there wasn't a facility to sell my work on the website.

Consequently, I put two recently completed oil paintings up for sale on the *New Art Portfolio* website. The first entitled *Cow in Hand,* which I'd painted during my last year at university, to advocate improved conditions and welfare for farm animals. And a second painting entitled *Global Food Distribution,* completed a few months later, advocating the abolition of poverty. Both sold within a couple of weeks for several hundred pounds each.

One of my first objectives was to gain publicity for my *Food for Thought* artwork, which I was now creating primarily for exhibitions rather than the website. One instance involved walking into the office of my local newspaper, *The Dagenham Post,* to arrange an appointment.

I wasn't expecting the reporter to see me there and then, which she did, I hadn't prepared anything to say and recall having a terrible hangover throughout the interview which however, can't have gone too badly because the following week, 31 January 2001, newspaper reporter Julie Russell had written a half-page article dedicated to my recent work with the heading *Brave New World for a Brave Artist*, accompanied with colour photographs of my paintings.

My first solo exhibition, entitled *Food for Thought*, was held at *Romford Central Library* in Essex, continuing the theme of animal welfare within the farming industry, which I ended up exhibiting at several venues around Essex during the early noughties.

Artwork created specifically to enhance the exhibitions included *Squashed Pig, Golden Fleece,* a second version of *Cow in Hand* (due to the first being sold) and an installation entitled *Golden Eggs* which attracted a lot of interest from the local press, one heading read *Artist is a Real Egghead* accompanied by a photograph of me with the top of my head missing, which I'm convinced had been digitally elongated to suggest I had an egg-shaped head.

The *Golden Eggs* installation highlighted how eggs laid by caged hens were (and still are) far cheaper to produce than free-range eggs.

Unfortunately, however, the price of such affordable goods results in hundreds of caged hens being forced to live cramped together in small confined spaces under artificial light, conditions where deadly diseases such as Salmonella can thrive. Hens are force fed an unnatural diet, denied exercise, beaks are burnt off to reduce pecking due to their extreme boredom and, when they fail to produce eggs regularly, are systematically slaughtered to be sold as dog food—all in the name of profit.

In preparation for my first solo exhibition, I decided to treat myself to a new pair of shoes for the preview evening and, after much contemplation, chose a pair of bright yellow plimsolls. During the last hectic few minutes prior to the show opening, to avoid leaving dirty footprints on the floor, I left my plimsolls on a small brown table in the foyer beneath a *Food for Thought* poster whilst making final touches to the display.

By now, members of the public had entered the building and I hastily returned to the foyer to put on my plimsolls where I noticed an elderly gentleman looking directly at them.

Initially, I wondered whether he was something to do with security. His eyes were fixed firmly on the plimsolls as he stroked his beard thoughtfully before declaring, somewhat victoriously, "I get it. They symbolise the carbon footprint of bananas!" Offering a wry smile as he walked off to view the other work on display.

To this day, I'm not entirely sure whether the elderly gentleman had an extremely dry sense of humour or genuinely believed my bright yellow plimsolls had been part of the show.

Prior to exhibiting work, many venues require an application form and a signed declaration of the content of work being proposed. *Chelmsford Central Library* responded to my application with a letter stating they were concerned with the content of my work in relation to health and safety regulations and, having read the description for my *Meat Dishes* which stated they are 'made from dead animal flesh' and the *Golden Eggs installation* 'consist of over three hundred egg shells depicting human faces and skulls', they would need more information before granting permission to exhibit the work.

I made a visit to the library and explained at the reception desk that the *Meat Dishes* were merely blown-up photographs from slides of the actual artwork that had been made from raw materials, including raw meat. The customer waiting behind me must have thought I was mad when she heard me protesting "—the yolks are made up of little human and skeleton faces and will be no threat whatsoever to the public."

She referred the issue to her manager and after several phone calls and much consultation and deliberation with councillors and health officials, the exhibition was eventually accepted.

After several exhibitions, Essex Council became aware of me and the content of my work and subsequent exhibitions were accepted without issue.

For example, I received a warm welcome from a helpful librarian at *Upminster Central Library* who showed great enthusiasm and interest in my artwork. During the hanging and installation of the show, which is the artist's responsibility at libraries, she was intrigued by the artefacts, offering assistance with the hanging and, on several occasions enquired about the meaning of my work and how they were made.

A Selection of *Food for Thought* Artwork.

A trader in farm animals sees only the commercial value, but not the unique beauty and nature of the animals.

Cow in Hand *(2000). Oil painting on wood, 100 cm x 75 cm.*

Focusing on the BSE crisis in the UK around the turn of the century (commonly referred to as *Mad Cow Disease*). Apparently cows were fed contaminated chopped up animal remains in a bid to artificially fatten them up, resulting in hundreds of thousands of cows being infected with the disease and subsequently killed before being burnt in mass graves to contain the spread of the disease.

Mad Cow Disease is yet another example of human interference causing environmental carnage which, incidentally put many farmers out of business and could have been avoided if we'd let nature take its course and allow cows to feed on their natural diet of grass and hay.

Golden Eggs *(2000). Mixed media installation, 120 cm x 90 cm x 25 cm.*

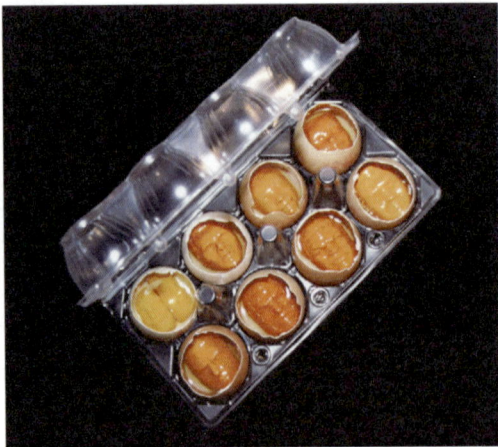

During my youth, I remember a famous advertising campaign promoting healthy eating that featured the slogan 'go to work on an egg' and the public were actively encouraged to eat a raw egg every day. However, I'm old enough to remember the Salmonella outbreak within the egg industry during the 1980s, resulting in an investigation that concluded one in four UK eggs contained the potentially deadly virus.

I first heard this disturbing news on the TV whilst tucking into my meal consisting of eggs, chips and beans, an experience I never quite got over and, twenty years later became the main inspiration for my *Golden Eggs* installation, consisting of three hundred and sixty chicken egg shells each accommodating a *yoke* covered in a clear epoxy resin, conveying either a human face or skeleton image—we are what we eat.

Global Food Distribution *(2001). Oil painting on wood, 70 cm x 60 cm.*

The work focuses on the disproportionate distribution of resources around the world that has resulted in vast areas of famine, starvation and poverty, coexisting in stark contrast with corporate millionaires and billionaires and the awful practice of legalised tax avoidance. Digitally enhanced versions of this painting were used as posters for the *Food for Thought* exhibitions.

Shakespeare's quote conveys the painting's narrative and served as my initial source of inspiration.

Surely, we would all starve were we to eat gravy with a spoon and peas with a knife.

Meat Dishes *(2000 -2001), 6 x Photographs, 37.5 cm x 37.5 cm.*

Representing farm animals set within an idyllic countryside setting. However, the *Meat Dish* animals are created from dead animal flesh. I took lots of *Meat Dish* photographs before they deteriorated, aware the natural decaying process grew visible after just a few days, by which time they'd become obsolete as a piece of artwork.

Consequently, there are no existing original *Meat Dishes,* all that remain are over a hundred 35mm slides and a few enlarged photographs that were used for the *Food for Thought* exhibitions.

The narrative aims to raise public awareness concerning what we're actually eating when purchasing food presented in a neat oblong shaped plastic tray covered in cellophane.

To maintain sales, the public are actively discouraged from confronting a more sinister truth that involves the ill treatment, abuse and brutal slaughter of sensitive, playful and intelligent creatures such as cows, chickens, pigs and sheep, often referred to as livestock, being unceremoniously slaughtered at abattoirs across the country. The *Meat Dishes* are raw, uncompromising images designed to shock with the impact of a sledgehammer.

Beef Holocaust I-IV *(2001). 4 x Oil painting on canvas, 50 cm x 40 cm.*

This series of four oil paintings convey the harrowing issue of poison within our livestock and how, in the name of *good* economic practise, the animals are treated. Because modern intensive farming relies on keeping a lot of animals confined together in small places, disease can run rampant. Consequently, livestock are fed ever-increasing amounts of antibiotics, which have resulted in the escalation of new antibiotic-resistant strains of virus being found in humans (particularly after consuming beef).

It's often overlooked how intelligent and sensitive cows actually are. As with humans, they respond positively to attention, play and affection. *Visiting Farms* are becoming ever increasingly popular and serve as an affordable and enjoyable day out for all the family, involving plenty of healthy exercise, useful for tiring out the kids and interaction between animals can be both educational and therapeutic and has proven to be an effective antidote to anxiety for all concerned.

Cow in Hand, 2nd version *(2002). Oil painting on canvas, 75 cm x 50 cm.*

Cows are gentle animals who are affectionate, emotional and intelligent. Gandhi described a cow as being "a poem of compassion."

In today's society, stress levels and mental health issues are reaching record levels, however interaction with cows at *visiting farms* are known to have a positive effect on people. Now that affordable plant-based foods are available in our supermarkets it is surely preferable such beautiful creatures live in harmony beside humans, serving as a form of mental therapy against the stresses of modern day living, rather than being sent on mass to an early and traumatic death in abattoirs.

Squashed Pig *(2002). Oil painting on wood, 70 cm x 60 cm.*

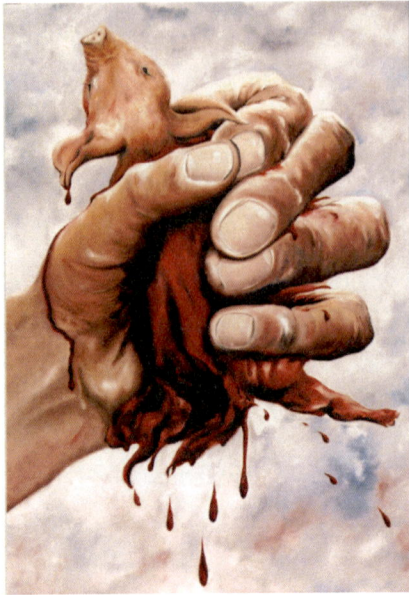

Pigs' natural habitat is woodland. In intelligence and awareness, they are equal to dogs and are extremely sociable creatures who live in family groups similar to that of humans.

To confine a dog permanently inside a cage that is too small to turn around in, would be considered by many as a grave act of vile cruelty, yet this is the standard treatment for mother pigs, who have their baby piglets forcibly taken away just twenty-four hours after they're born. So when you're next in a supermarket aisle looking for a carton of dead animal flesh wrapped in cellophane, it's worth remembering there's always an alternative *meat free* choice in the next aisle.

Charcoal Pig *(2003).* Charcoal on A4 cartridge paper.

I remember drawing this image on a day out with the family at a *city farm* in London. The pigs were so friendly and just loved being stroked, however, they had a rather pungent smell which remained on your hand after stroking them.

On our way home, the children insisted on opening the car windows due to an awful smell in the car. I asked everyone to check under their shoes then suddenly realised as I rubbed my nose, the awful stench was on my hand which, unfortunately, everyone had to endure throughout the drive home. *Charcoal Pig* took no more than a couple of minutes to complete in my sketchbook. I like its rawness and spontaneous quality, completely different to how I usually approach my work.

Golden Fleece *(2003). Oil painting on canvas, 75 cm x 50 cm.*

In the UK, sheep are regularly dipped and sprayed with chemicals to protect them from external parasites and disease. However, the dip formulae contains synthetic parathyroids that, although considered safe for the farmer, are extremely toxic and frequently discarded into local streams and rivers causing the mass destruction of natural wildlife, particularly fish, birds and insects within the area, which often remains uninhabitable for many years after.

Sheep at Night *(2004)*, Digitally enhanced version of *Golden Fleece*.

Sheep at Night was one of many digitally enhanced images created for the *Food for Thought* project. Developed from the painting *Golden Fleece*, which in turn was created from sketches I'd made during my visit to a *city farm* in London.

Influences Food for Thought incorporates much media experimentation to convey its fundamental message of animal welfare within the agricultural industry. Influences for the work include artist Chris Olifi's piece entitled *No Woman No Cry*, which conveys a strong and emotional message through experimentation with mixed media (as mentioned in the previous chapter).

Several paintings, such as *Cow in Hand* and *Squashed Pig* are influenced by Surrealism, playing with perspective and scale with animal figures, placed out of their natural settings and subject to overbearing human oppression in the form of a disproportionately large human hand.

The *Golden Eggs* installation had been described as *surreal* in comment books by spectators during exhibitions. Consisting of 360 chicken egg shells containing plaster cast faces and skulls that replace the conventional yolks, to convey the serious issue of human interference within our food chain resulting in disease and ill health.

The installation is designed to convey a contemporary social message rather than exercise freedom of thought through dreams or autonomy and therefore I regard the piece as *contemporary* rather than *Surreal*.

The *Food for Thought* project successfully raised public awareness (and still does) concerning animal welfare within the agricultural industry. Using a variety of iconic graphic images, supported by accurately sourced information. Yet there is little content that offers solutions and alternatives to the deplorable treatment of farm animals.

It is, therefore, important to recognise that many farmers *do* take the welfare of their animals seriously, which fundamentally conflicts with the pressures involved in maintaining economic survival. According to a BBC report in 2023, 94% of farmers under the age of forty raised mental health concerns, naming *cost of living, Brexit* and the *Covid pandemic* as the main reasons. The report also confirmed there had been 'thirty-six suicides in the UK last year.'

In response to such disturbing information, I believe the following changes within the agricultural industry would reduce emotional and financial stress for the vast majority of farmers and their associated workforce and secure the industries' economic security for the twenty-first century and beyond:

With the recent dramatic increase in public demand, livestock farms can cost effectively be converted to grow and produce plant-based goods. Many livestock farms can be converted into nature reserves with areas for reforestation. Many farms would make ideal leisure venues, offering families the chance to interact with the animals in a more natural setting. Improve revenue with themed rides, restaurants and relevant entertainment such as art classes and topical presentations to help improve public awareness concerning animal and environmental welfare.

The war between Russia and Ukraine has created an international energy crisis, resulting in dramatic fuel price increases, highlighting the need for self-sustainable carbon friendly renewable energy and virtually all farmland is potentially suitable terrain for much needed solar farms. Government support and investment would be vital to ensure the success of such an ambitious change in agricultural policy, for example, farming subsidies given by the EU would have to be reinstated.

Throughout the creation of *Food for Thought,* I was fully committed to what I was doing. I was dedicated and believed passionately in the cause and what it was saying. A lot of the work incorporates death, decay and deterioration, however, I was in the zone and enjoyed creating pioneering artwork to support animal rights, a cause I passionately believed in (and still do). New ideas were constantly entering my head and my priority was to write them down on paper and develop the ideas in the best possible way.

During the process of creating the *Meat Dishes,* I was working with dead animal flesh whilst advocating their welfare, which, on reflection, is a paradox. The artwork was rotting during the process of its creation and consequently only lasted a few days, which is why I took hundreds of slides.

I submitted several *Meat Dish* slides to DEFRA (Department for Environment Food & Rural Affairs), to ask whether they'd consider using the images for any future publications. Shortly after sending the proposal, it dawned on me how an organisation concerned with animal welfare might actually be offended by receiving images of dead animal flesh.

So when the response arrived (by post in those days), I was not just happy but also a little relieved, to receive a wonderful in-depth reply from DEFRA's director, saying how he enjoyed viewing the *Meat Dishes* and thought they were *innovative* and conveyed a powerful message. He encouraged me to continue with my work but declined using the *Meat Dishes,* which, on reflection, I can understand how DEFRA's ethical competence could have been compromised were they to use artwork made from dead animals.

During this period I became a full member of the *AoI (Association of Illustration)*, with whom I participated in a London Exhibition held by the *Sheridan Russell Gallery*, featuring three original watercolours which incidentally, I've never put up for sale and an illustration framed and donated for the charity *Paintings in Hospitals*, which I assume is hanging somewhere on an NHS hospital wall in a children's ward.

I wrote to loads of Illustration Agencies enclosing either slides or a disc containing examples of my work. Virtually all responses contained the word 'unfortunately', which is what I'd look out for rather than waste time reading the full reply. *Allied Artists* and *Emotional Rescue* were interested in my work and *the Central Illustration Agency (CIA)* offered me a workplace.

However, I soon realised how competitive the industry could be and I struggled with restrictive briefs and tight budgets that were driven by deadlines involving sleep deprivation. We were constantly encouraged to maintain high competitive fees using guidelines provided in order to avoid a 'race to the bottom'.

Unfortunately, the illustrator offering the most affordable work usually won the commission. I mainly worked freelance and had some success receiving commissions for book covers and a series of health & safety brochures, for example illustrating how to lift goods safely.

My Illustration Portfolio contains a variety of themed work, each presented in folders, including *Advertising, Alternative Portraits, Book Covers, Information* and a *Young Adults* folder predominantly comprising of *Horror and Romance* genres that targeted stereotypical teenage interests. For example, several romantic images were designed to suggest an exciting love story, developed from photographs overlaid with flat colours via *Photoshop* to give a bright *pop-art* effect that would appeal to a teenager.

The *Advertising* section of my portfolio also relies heavily on digitally enhanced images. For example, I use the same photograph (which happens to be my dear wife Lynne), to promote two entirely opposing messages. One is advertising an alcoholic beverage, and the other warning about the dangers of alcohol abuse.

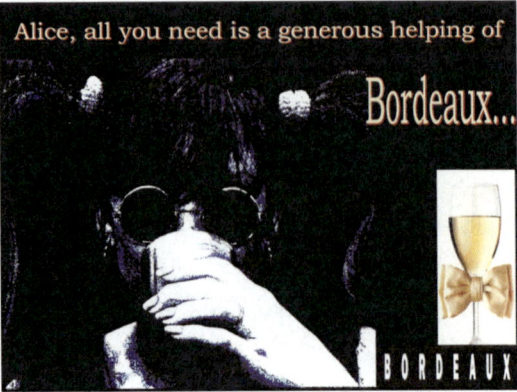

Alice, all you need is a generous helping of **Bordeaux...**

BORDEAUX

TEENAGE 'BINGE' DRINKING

THE NEW REVOLUTION

05 Distance Between Land and Sea

By 2003, I'd commenced work on a new project entitled *The Distance Between Land and Sea,* whilst continuing to promote *Food for Thought* artwork to agencies, publishers, newspapers and anyone concerned with animal welfare.

The Distance Between Land and Sea project consists of a collection of large seascape paintings to convey issues concerning global climate change and associated man-made pollution, including excessive carbon emissions, which is now constantly covered in today's news.

However, a couple of decades ago when these paintings were created, such views were considered by some meteorologists and most government scientists, as mere hypothetical theories rather than a proven phenomenon and were generally dismissed as a hindrance to powerful energy organisations that strengthened the economy and gave shareholders, including governments, large profits.

I approached this project fully aware that at least half the public were sceptical of the relatively new phenomenon referred to as *global warming*. And so I incorporated a somewhat fractious beauty within the content of my work to make the horrendous truth appear almost palatable through iconic content.

For example, much of the seascapes include dark elements such as sunken boats, dead trees, thunderous clouds and clenched fists, often however, juxtaposed with beautiful sunsets, dramatic skies and sun-drenched waves sometimes adorned with an example of our precious sea life.

Such compositions were not merely for aesthetic purposes alone, they were to convey both the wonder and horror involved with preserving our fragile environment, which are basically two very different sides of the same coin—Viewing the land from the sea and viewing the sea from the land, will give you two entirely different pictures from the same scene.

The objective of my project was simply to raise public awareness concerning rising sea levels, resulting in eroding coastlines that were capable of consuming properties. The increasing frequency of extreme weather involving storms, cyclones, heatwaves, droughts and flooding were and remain, a scientifically based categoric fact and it's important we all, as climate campaigner Greta Thunberg says, "Listen to the science."

I enjoy oil painting and know exactly why artists prefer such a medium. They are very tactile have a unique smell and are forgiving when mistakes are made due to remaining wet for hours after application. Any effect, colour, texture and mood can be attained with oils. I would spend many hours in my studio working on each painting, never compromising on quality to meet deadlines.

I also dedicated a lot of time researching the subject to help reach a deeper understanding of the issues concerned. I believe subject knowledge serves as important criteria in creating quality work for a project, for it is necessary to know exactly what the paintings are saying prior to releasing them into the public domain, whether for publication, exhibition or online galleries.

The noughties were happy days. We were strong as a family and Lynne appeared content and fulfilled, devoting much of her time to raising the boys and making sure everyone was happy, whilst I committed long laborious hours to painting, often until late in the evening.

Lynne and I had become aware of how quiet the boys were in the company of others and didn't seem to make friends naturally. Every *parents' evening*, where we met their teachers, we'd be advised how quiet they were and so we persuaded them both to join clubs involving group activities such as football, athletics, badminton, judo and swimming. And at home I taught them how to play an old football game called *Subbuteo* that I'd kept since I was a child.

Over several years, we held many well organised *Subbuteo* tournaments that were treated very seriously by all concerned. I seem to remember Christopher steadily grew better with each tournament and during the latter years won all the competitions.

When I wasn't painting, my role with the family could be described as *Extra-Curricular Activities & Leisure Manager*. We frequently went on days out to safari parks, adventure theme parks, visited castles, festivals, funfairs and many other attractive locations and often took weekend breaks and holidays for a week or two abroad or stayed at holiday camps such as *Pontins* in Blackpool.

On one occasion, at *Knowsley Safari Park,* we entered the monkey area and almost immediately they began jumping on our bonnet, which we all thought was hilarious. However, the mood soon changed from laughter to horror when they started to rip off any rubber they could find attached to the car. First the window wipers were stripped off as the monkey sat on the bonnet peering into our window screen, somewhat satisfied with our outraged reaction.

We'd changed from smiling at the cheeky little beasts to screaming "get the f**k off!". One particular monkey wasn't at all perturbed and continued to strip the rubber that surrounded our front window.

By this time, we were all rolling around inside the car screaming for him to leave us alone. Defiantly, the monkey took a longer deliberate look into our car, seemingly amused, perhaps even gloating at the humans' strange and erratic behaviour concerning his actions. Eventually, I managed to put the car in reverse and make a hasty retreat backwards out of the monkey area.

Distance Between Land and Sea highlights the disturbing issue of *global warming* and subsequent rising sea levels and extreme weather involving heat waves, flooding, droughts and wildfires running rampant across the countryside, which has recently been referred to as *climate chaos*.

Whilst creating the *Distance* paintings global warming was a contentious issue and dismissed from being a real and genuine threat to life on our planet by many respected scientists who, through government reports published by the media, regarded recent excessive weather patterns as being merely a *blip* and nothing of undue concern.

However, following unprecedented records involving excessively high temperatures, rising sea levels, droughts and rainfalls, it is now generally accepted that unless we dramatically reduce carbon emissions, the ecological system will collapse and destroy life's feeding chain, resulting in millions of species becoming extinct. Scientists now warn that global warming is causing land to lose nutrition and crops to fail, resulting in mass starvation, global poverty and enforced migration and millions of premature deaths.

Related environmental issues include the mass volume of pollution entering our freshwater rivers, lakes and seaside resorts in the form of raw sewage, pesticides and plastic fibres. Largely as a result of the ludicrous decision to privatise water in the UK during the 1980s, which left companies feeling obliged to prioritise profit over investment within the infrastructure, resulting in twenty percent of water supplies leaking daily into the streets, preventing swimming groups, families and even your pet dog from enjoying a swim in a lake or at the seaside due to the risk of becoming seriously ill by disease.

Such regular deposits of pollution are already having a devastating effect on our natural wildlife, particularly insects and fish that are crucial to the ecological balance of our food chain.

The *Distance* paintings were commercially successful and all the paintings have been sold into private collections. First exhibited as a themed collection of work in 2007 at the final *Liverpool Academy of Arts* public event prior to the building being demolished in preparation for the *European Capital City of Culture,* which occurred the following year.

The paintings sold well through online platforms such as *Art-Gallery-UK, Fine-Art-America and Saatchi Online and* were last exhibited in 2011 during my second show at *The Malvern Heights Theatre,* organised by the directors of *Art-*

Gallery-UK, Aileen and Mike and Mitchell. They were a married couple who took a huge gamble by leaving well-paid jobs to buy the *Art-Gallery-UK* domain name, which they've since developed into a highly successful online selling platform for both new and established artists.

Aileen would liaise with artists and customers regarding their queries and concerns, whereas Mike concentrated on admin work behind the scenes. Aileen was always available on her personal phone, which I appreciated and respected, as this was not always the case with other selling platforms.

In 2009, I arranged with Aileen to collect my work following my first exhibition at *The Malvern Heights.* When Lynne and I arrived at the theatre, after travelling the four-hour journey from Derbyshire, there was no sign of my artwork anywhere!

I asked what had happened to my paintings at the reception desk and nobody seemed to have a clue. I phoned Aileen and she calmed me down before advising "all is well" advising my paintings had been shipped to Douglas on the Isle of Mann for an exhibition. "You could have told me," I said, but was immediately appeased by being informed several of my paintings had just sold and how they were hoping to continue the "good run" on the Isle of Mann.

I couldn't keep up with where my *Distance* paintings were and hadn't seen them for several months when I contacted the Isle of Mann venue, which was a hotel, only to be told they'd been shipped out somewhere, where exactly they did not know.

Again I contacted Aileen to raise my concern, emphasising they were my 'life's work', an exaggeration I know but they did take over five-hundred hours to complete through sweat, inspiration and dedication. She interrupted to explain how they needed the work to help fulfil contracts made with exhibition organisers around the country, I rather tentatively agreed with their plans before ending the call. At least she was communicating with me, I thought, *If she wanted to run off with my paintings, she wouldn't be wasting her time talking to me over the phone.*

When you've created an impressive piece of work or exciting new project, after researching the subject and developing sketches and roughs, through hours of hard work and dedication and you finally arrive with a new and unique finished product. The process of selling can be like wrapping up a newly born baby inside a cotton blanket and leaving it outside of the church steps.

Eventually, on the twenty-seventh December 2009, a massive box arrived at the door containing the remaining paintings from my series of *Distance* work. I hadn't seen my babies for months and had no idea where they'd been until I noticed the paintings were covered in bubble wrap with tape marked 'Edinburgh Art Fair' which, to this day, I haven't got round to add onto my *exhibitions* portfolio list.

A Selection of *Distance Between Land and Sea* paintings.

Art is not a mere form of knowledge or ideology. Above all, it is creation—both realism and non-realism are creative facts. Essentially, there is no distance between land & sea.

81

Lost at Sea l & ll *(2003). Oil on canvas. 80 cm x 60 cm each.*

 The first painting incorporates a rather simplified relationship between colour and form to convey a sailing boat in difficulty with the skipper apparently struggling to remain afloat and conveys a sense of danger. The vibrant orange sky suggests an impending heatwave. The second painting suggests the boat has eventually made it back to shore, however, the condition and circumstances remain ambivalent.

The initial inspiration for the painting came during a day out with the family somewhere on the beautiful south coast of Spain, when I came across a similar semi-sunken boat in an estuary. She was old and dilapidated, semi-submerged and had obviously seen better days. She looked neglected and forgotten and I couldn't help wondering if only she could disclose her history, experiences and secrets, oh what a tale she would tell.

Mourning Spring *(2003). Oil on canvas. 80 cm x 60 cm.*

I'd thought of the title *Mourning Spring* well before making any sketches for the painting, which is a play on words suggesting our seasons may become somewhat melancholic. During the planning stage, I attempted to incorporate an alternative view of springtime—a post-apocalyptic spring.

The painting incorporates visual metaphors relating to the death of our environment, with three elements competing as the main focal point: The stylised tree in the foreground, influenced by Roger Dean's iconic twisted trees that you can see in his marvellous book *Views*, representing the reaper and a sense of impending doom. The mid-distance depicts an aquatic funeral in the form of a sunken *deceased* boat and visiting *hearse*. The pale moon in the far distance represents somewhere out of this world, perhaps the afterlife.

Winter Heatwave *(2004). Oil on canvas. 80 cm x 60 cm.*

The devastating effects of global warming are now evident in the form of ever-increasing floods within villages, towns and cities in every continent, resulting in the mass destruction of crops, homelessness, poverty and a dramatic rise in disease. The composition evokes an intense heat, portraying dead trees with their reflection smouldering within a lifeless, uninhabitable surrounding.

Although the painting conveys a somewhat morbid prophecy, I believe the image maintains an iconic quality that will encourage the viewer to embrace the sincere message and, ultimately, raise awareness of climate change and the potentially catastrophic consequences. The tree branches that serve as the main focal point of the piece were developed from a photograph taken during a holiday in the beautiful country of Spain, vibrant colours were added to support the narrative of climate change and convey intense heat.

The Piano Blues *(2005). Oil on canvas. 80 cm x 60 cm.*

We're all going to be feeling the blues when our pianos are swept away by the rising sea. *The Piano Blues* is a shoreline scene with a quirky edge to it. The narrative incorporates an abandoned piano drifting from the shore. Originally, the piano was designed for an album cover during my Illustration period, which, unfortunately, never materialised.

By this time, I wanted to create more paintings to support my *Distance* exhibitions and, being resourceful, I sketched the piano design onto a large canvas and developed the composition into a *climate change* scene involving this grand old musical instrument being surrounded, rather precariously, by a relentless and unforgiving incoming sea.

Rock Guitar *(2005). Oil on canvas. 80 cm x 60 cm.*

The composition involves a guitar shaped rock protruding from the sea, embedded naturally into the surrounding environment. Developed from a guitar shaped sculpture I'd made using clay, inspired by Dame Barbara Hepworth's remarkable work. Particularly, her semi-abstract sculptures such as *Wave* (1943) and *Pelagos* (1946) that incorporate beautiful smooth and fluid contours that demonstrated her passion for nature.

My sculpture eventually decomposed due to not having been fired in a kiln. However, the ageing process produced some interesting results involving transition and its ultimate demise, consequently photographs I'd taken during this natural decaying process proved invaluable as reference for depicting a natural, organic looking guitar shaped rock.

Twisted Nature *(2006). Oil on canvas. 80 cm x 60 cm.*

Global climate change has caused ever-increasing severe weather patterns, with reports of tornadoes occurring more frequently around the globe. People are paid to follow tornadoes in a bid to identify their traits, what series of meteorological effects cause them to occur and why are they increasing in frequency and velocity?

Storm chaser: "I love witnessing the savage beauty of a tornado in its natural environment, such as the sweeping prairies of Oklahoma."

There is something mesmerising and quite iconic about the sight of a tornado, however such natural beauty can be dangerous, for example on 26 April 1989, the deadliest tornado in Bangladesh's history ripped through the cities of Daulatpur and Saturia, killing well over a thousand people.

Whirlwind Romance *(2006). Oil on canvas. 80 cm x 60 cm.*

Conveying the catastrophic effect of global warming within a somewhat satirical context. I've heard many people proclaim, in a rather self-satisfied manner, how they enjoy the ever increasingly hot summers, apparently completely oblivious to the ever-increasing carbon emissions. Such irreversible and devastating consequences will end a short-lived *burning-hot* honeymoon.

Stop Whaling *(2007). Oil on canvas. 80 cm x 60 cm.*

The disproportionately large hand can be perceived as either saving or destroying the whale, the outcome is for you to decide. There are Surreal elements contained within the painting *Stop Whaling*, however the narrative is profoundly contemporary and the message is within the title.

I believe it is barbaric and highly immoral for humans to kill any natural wildlife, whether for fun, sport, to inhabit their natural territory or make an economic profit from their bodies, such as their skin, flesh, fur, ivory or fins. It is imperative we respect and protect nature and the beautiful creatures that are equally entitled to live in peace and harmony with humans on this unique and wonderful planet.

Unfortunately, the human species appear to have an inherent burning desire to systematically destroy their surrounding environment for short-term economic gain, apparently ignorant to the need for nature to thrive in order to preserve their own survival.

Whales are highly intelligent and sensitive creatures that suffer agonisingly slow deaths when hunted by fishing trawlers. The long and tortuous process involves hours of stalking in the sea, which involves being harpooned multiple times and when caught they're butchered whilst still alive, a process that can take several hours.

Wish You Were Here *(2007). Oil on canvas. 80 cm x 60 cm.*

The fish is alive only because they are a fish out of water. My aim was to make the clouds and surrounding area appear cold and uninhabitable in order to convey the magnitude of a pending environmental disaster involving oil, chemical waste, sewage, plastic, cans, old nets and many other discarded materials that are destroying our natural and beautiful oceans and the millions of wonderful species living there.

Unfortunately, many species have become extinct in recent years with many more destined to follow unless our habits change dramatically.

06 A Surreal Impression

When I'm not painting, visiting art galleries and museums is a favourite pastime of mine. When I lived on the outskirts of London, it was just a matter of hopping into the city by car or tube, where there is a rich and diverse choice of venues to visit featuring historic and contemporary art collections, the majority of which are free to visit.

It has always interested me how art through the centuries has produced vastly different styles, genres and themes. And how social etiquette and moral values have changed through the centuries. For example, obesity was once considered a sign of affluence and wealth in western culture and royal artists were obliged to exaggerate the size of noble subjects in their paintings. Now, however, historians are left questioning whether people of notoriety, such as Henry VIII, were actually as large as their portraits suggest.

Paintings in galleries consist of many different cultures and eras involving faith, dress, rituals and the social climate of the time. Many examples of artwork from different periods and movements can be viewed on the same day in a single building, where authentic paintings created by *Romantics, Impressionists, Surrealists, Cubists, Expressionists,*

Modernists and *Postmodernists* convey a diverse array of narrative, style, media, texture and sometimes magic.

Such artwork is often displayed inside beautiful buildings that possess architectural style, grandeur and heritage in their own right. I have enjoyed many wonderful hours in London galleries and museums over the years and other cities, including a memorable experience viewing a large collection of Vincent Van Gogh's work at *Van Gogh's Museum* in Amsterdam.

Such experiences have inscribed a deep impression on me as a person and have subsequently influenced my outlook on art and its entwined relationship with society.

Ever since the invention of the photographic image, around 1835, visual artists have felt obliged to find a new role as opposed to painting realistic portraits or landscapes that the photograph could do perfectly well instantaneously and without any particular need for creative ability.

Impressionists were the first art movement to respond by painting everyday scenes in the *en plein air* (open air), depicting average everyday people working or socialising, rather than classic fine art compositions involving grandeur and the aristocracy. They incorporated human imagination in a new, revolutionary style that involved slapping on paint in a physical, gestural way with an emphasis on immediacy and the brushstroke, which served as a fresh alternative to photographic realism.

Impressionism developed from a group of young artists who began to work and socialise together during the eighteen-seventies in Paris, where their first official exhibition was held in 1874. Founder member, Claude Monet's painting entitled *Impression Sunrise,* 1874, is often credited as the painting that gave the movement its name when art critic Louis Leroy criticised the painting in a news article, describing the 'loose and quickly applied brushwork' as merely an 'impression of a sunrise'.

Such criticism however, was endorsed by the rebellious young artists and they accepted the name with enthusiastic defiance against the art establishment who, at the time, considered Impressionism as rather vulgar, preferring traditional tried and tested conventional painting techniques that aspired to realistic representation and grand themes such as mysticism, religion and nobility.

Founder members of Impressionism include Cassatt, Degas, Manet, Monet, Morisot, Pisarro and Renoir. Mary Cassatt was born in America, where she received formal training at the *Pennsylvanian Academy of Fine Arts* and continued her studies in France and Italy before settling in Paris in 1874. She regularly showed work locally at the salons and became acquainted with Edgar Dagas, who invited her to join the group of independent artists, later known as the Impressionists.

Mary Cassatt and Berthe Morisot had the most difficult path to becoming self-sustainable professional artists. Being female, they were restricted from practising *open air* painting due to contemporary social etiquette that dictated women had to be escorted by a man when in public. Today, such misogynistic views are considered utterly unacceptable and illegal, being discriminatory and in the UK breaches the equality act (2010).

The Impressionists were founded approximately forty-five years prior to women gaining the right to vote, however despite such restrictions, Mary Cassatt had become an internationally recognised artist after the growing popularity of Impressionism towards the end of the nineteenth century when she painted *The Boating Party*, 1893 and completed the mural *Modern Woman*, commissioned for the Woman's Building at Chicago's *World's Columbian Exposition* to celebrate the 400th anniversary of Christopher Columbus's arrival.

During my time at university, I was introduced to examples of Picasso's *anti-war* art, which I found thoroughly inspiring regarding the potential power of narrative art and have returned to his work many times since. His early work was affected following the death of a close friend and consequently developed a sombre tone known as his *Blue Period.*

After meeting his first true love, Fernande Olivier, he developed a new, more uplifting style referred to as his *Rose Period and* later became interested in African art, particularly their sculptures and masks and during this period created *Les Demoiselles d'Avignon (The Young Ladies of Avignon),* 1907, which broke all the rules of art.

He worked tirelessly for several months, making hundreds of sketches and plans in preparation for the painting. The semi-abstract composition incorporates a structural clarity using simplified forms that convey nude figures, two wearing African designed masks.

The composition ignores conventional perspective and vanishing points, a process never previously seen, which he developed in his later Cubist work and, after initially receiving a sceptical response from both art critics and colleagues, the painting was eventually exhibited several years later and is now generally considered to be his first internationally recognised masterpiece.

Picasso was not afraid to push boundaries and work outside of his comfort zone, to create and develop pioneering styles and techniques which he used to great effect in achieving a balance between realism and abstraction. Other African influenced work include *Bust of a Woman, Mother and Child, Nude with Raised Arms* and *Three Women.*

With the arrival of the photograph, new alternative and pioneering ideas became the artist's obsession, an ideology that is advocated within the art world to this day. For example, several course lecturers, during my time at university, considered oil painting to be *old-school and* was frowned upon for being *too conventional* and failing to be *inventive* and *original.*

My personal view is that inventiveness and originality can be achieved regardless of the media being used, whether it's paint, charcoal, plaster, bronze, digital, mixed media, elephant dung or anything else, it's the artwork's narrative content rather than the media being used that takes precedence.

Another equally intriguing discussion concerning so-called *good* art focuses on the concept of abstraction, considered by many to be a relatively new ground-breaking and alternative way of seeing, to achieve deep personal and emotional concepts and thoughts. In contrast, others regard abstract images as being little more than aesthetically decorative.

Of course, there is no right or wrong answer and whether art is *good* or not is entirely subjective. However, such discussions can be thought-provoking and serve as an opportunity for anyone interested in art, whether an academic or practitioner, develop a deeper understanding concerning different visual styles and genres.

Reading and understanding art history, pioneering movements, styles and philosophies from different times within the world, has played an important role in the development of my practical work. Reminiscent of jazz musicians who stray from the original music score during a live performance, resulting in an inspirational solo that is unique, crazy and beautiful. Yet such magic can only be achieved if the musician knows exactly how to play the song's chords in its original format before attempting to elaborate with their personalised rendition.

I have read many books that talk about art movements, their origins, ideology, style and motivation. And discovered how new movements, particularly during the last century, offered a new alternative way of thinking, through literature and art, to a discontented society. Several developed after the First World War when people felt dejected and let down, believing poor government decisions resulted in the unnecessary deaths of millions of young men and were responsible for mass poverty.

Artists, who were also members of the public, also grew disillusioned with authority and the establishment, out of which art movements rose, such as the anarchic *Dadaists* who were the original punk rockers of the time, known for enjoying wild debauched parties.

Prior to some *Dada* exhibitions, visitors were given hatchets and invited to express their opinions in a bid to articulate an angry enthusiasm for destroying the past. From this radical anti-establishment movement came the more intellectually aware *Surrealists*, founded by Andre Breton, who created the first Surrealist manifesto followed by their own newspaper entitled *La Revolution Surrealiste*.

They were inspired by dreams and placed normal, everyday items into unusual or absurd settings. Their objective was to totally liberate the mind and release the subconscious.

Surrealists wanted to liberate art from all ties with history and the Greek-Roman renaissance. They pioneered the process of automatic writing, which involved putting down random thoughts that came to mind by ignoring all constraints such as censorship. Visual artists adopted a similar strategy and frequently used ephemeral rubbish to create collages.

Surreal paintings encompass a wide variety of styles, some of which are quite abstract and I personally don't understand the message (if anything) they are trying to convey. I regard autonomous writing and drawing to be more of an experience or event and, by definition, the content is abstract and completely aloof from social concerns, which, perhaps this is their message.

In my view, successful Surrealism achieves a balance between reality and abstraction, examples include Rene Magritte's thought-provoking painting *The Treachery of Images*, 1929, depicting a smoker's pipe with accompanying text stating 'Cesi n'est une pipe' (This is not a pipe) and appears to contradict the content of the image.

Magritte offered an explanation for his controversial work, saying, "The famous pipe. How people reproached me for it! And yet, could you stuff my pipe? No, it's just a representation, is it not? So if I had written 'This is a pipe', I'd have been lying!"

Salvador Dali's *La persistència de la memòria (The Persistence of Memory)*, 1931, consist of melted clocks used as symbols to express the concept of timeless time, ideas which had recently arisen out of Einstein's contemporary theories of relativity, most of which have since been proven accurate. Albert Einstein frequently advocated the importance of art, for example, when he stated, "Imagination is more important than knowledge. Knowledge is limited. Imagination encircles the world."

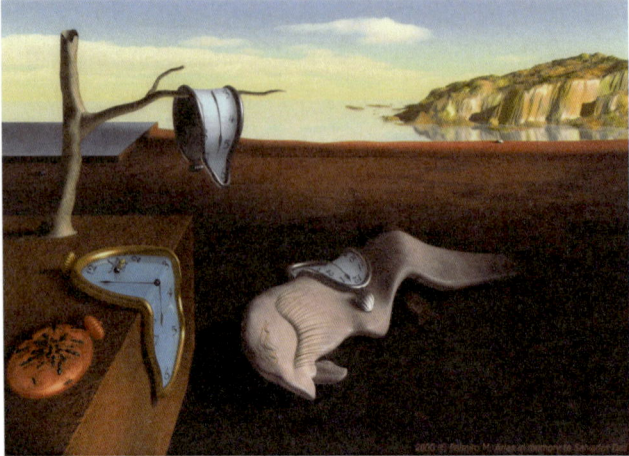

Artists have created alternative, often idealistic, worlds as a source of escapism such as the *Romantics* and in more recent times Roger Dean, who became famous when nineteen-seventies progressive rock bands such as *Yes* used his artwork for their album covers. Several of which I bought for their artwork rather than the music, including the albums *Yesterdays* and *Close to the Edge.* He was the first artist who made a powerful impression on me when I was a teenager and I had several of his posters on my bedroom wall.

Roger Dean is a specialist with an airbrush who created beautiful intricate and realistic fantasy worlds containing organic-like buildings, mythical creatures and fish floating in the air, with flawlessly smooth skies and backgrounds that omitted any sign of a brushstroke. In his book *Views,* I read how he'd once tried painting with oils but hated the experience, which he describes as "working with mud."

The book contains a section focusing on his interest in design and contains examples of his pioneering architecture involving homes built predominantly underground that coexist with the natural environment, rather than disrupt nature and the beautiful countryside. Such conceptual revolutionary designs, created during the nineteen-seventies, were environmentally friendly and well ahead of their time.

New art movements and pioneering ideas are constantly arising. For example, during the bidding for a painting by Banksy entitled *Girl With Balloon* (present academic consensus favours the belief the work was created in 2006).

A guillotine shredded the extremely valuable painting in full view of shocked bidders who, with phones in their hands and mouths on the floor, were offering over a million pounds for the piece. Needless to say the publicity stunt worked and the guillotined artwork, now called *Love is in the Bin*, 2018, is worth far more than it was prior to the outrageous public performance.

A lot of Banksy's artwork incorporates thought-provoking social commentary to highlight a powerful contemporary message, such as *Flower Thrower,* 2003, depicting a rioter throwing a bunch of flowers, as opposed to a conventional petrol bomb. *Slave Labour,* 2012, highlights the appalling and illegal practice of children working long hours in atrocious conditions for extremely low pay.

Kissing Coppers, 2004, dispels the stereotypical myth that all police officers are white, macho, heterosexual males. And *Show me the Monet,* 2005, satirises the famous painting *The Water Lily Pond,* 1899, by Impressionist Claude Monet, highlighting the contemporary problem of pollution and fly-tipping in our rivers, by superimposing discarded items such as a traffic cone and shopping trolleys protruding out of Monet's original lily pond.

Much of Banksy's work conveys social and political issues that often expose injustice and nonsensical norms within our society. His work undoubtedly flirts with controversy, which is largely overcome by his use of profound satire and humour, which empowers the sometimes dark nature of his graphic images, enabling the artwork to become accessible and appreciated by the general public.

Banksy's artwork is fundamentally inclusive, encouraging people to engage and debate, who may otherwise have felt resigned or disconnected with such issues. His satirical social commentary has certainly influenced my approach to work, particularly regarding the importance of maintaining an element of humour when conveying potentially heavy contemporary issues. For example, my *Golden Eggs* installation highlights serious public health and animal welfare concerns, however, during exhibitions I've often caught spectators looking at the work with a bemused smile on their face.

Digital art is a relatively new media that can reproduce all the above, virtually. However, digital artwork can lack spontaneity and authenticity and in many cases tangibility.

In contrast, paint is a tactile substance the artist can indulge in by physically immersing in the pigment. Many are inclined to throw, drip and pour paint over their canvas, some are more likely to roll around in the stuff and stick their fingers in the paint to feel and appreciate the texture. Add sand, glue, sawdust or anything else imaginable to create something original, unique and tangible.

Digital art is the latest string to the artist's bow, that I'm not averse to experimenting with myself. For example, *Midnight Sheep* is a digitally enhanced version of the oil painting *Golden Fleece* from the *Food for Thought* project and, at the time of writing, are both being showcased online by various hosts. I am also presently working on a portrait image that metamorphoses digitally in four stages, entitled *Savage Hallucination,* which I'll discuss in more detail later.

Artists have always used new found materials and resources to create unique and innovative artwork. One new source of inspiration occurred with the invention of cine film and before that the camera. Going back further, artists discovered screen-prints, wood etchings, the ability to smelt bronze and iron.

Beautiful sculptures were made during the stone age, including Stonehenge, amongst many other fine examples of stone circles. Pyramids built thousands of years ago are wonderful and mysterious works of architecture containing equally impressive artefacts which, at the time of building, were the result of brand new state-of-the-art technology.

In fact, man has been creating ever since he learnt to make a mark on a rock or scribe using the remains of a burnt twig from the previous night's fire, which we now refer to as *charcoal*.

07 Class

Sometime during 2010. I'd just finished cleaning up after a painting session, feeling somewhat underwhelmed regarding the progression of my work. I could hear the radio in the background and the host's relentless bombardment of small talk about the weather and light-hearted jibes bitching about celebrities and their choice of garment for a major showbiz function the previous night.

I'd just finished drying the paintbrushes when I noticed a shabby-looking reference book lying in the corner. I opened the cover to be greeted by hundreds of old 35mm slides, including several pages of *Meat Dishes* from the *Food for Thought* project. I removed one and held it to the light. The slide revealed an idyllic countryside scene depicting a cow grazing leisurely in a field.

However, on closer inspection, the cow was created from the flesh of a dead chicken; the field was made from mushy peas, a mashed potato sky and a chicken egg yolk represented a beautiful summer's day.

My initial gut reaction was disgust. 'What a sick collection of slides, the best place for them is straight in the bin!'

As I returned the slide I composed my thoughts, 'Of course they're horrible, they were designed to be horrible, to raise public awareness concerning the mistreatment of beautiful, sensitive and intelligent animals, in this case a cow, bred purely to endure a short and horrendous life prior to being brutally murdered in an abattoir.'

I returned the book to its shelf thinking it was a shame they were hidden away, gathering dust and then it suddenly came to me, a slide presentation showcasing my innovative *Meat Dishes* would be a great opportunity to educate students on animal welfare whilst introducing them to examples of *mixed media art*. I needed a new challenge and the prospect of delivering a presentation excited me.

I forgot about my momentary aspiration to teach for several weeks until, on my way home after hanging a small exhibition at a local library, on impulse, I walked into my local junior school, *The Green,* to enquire about doing support work for one day a week, emphasising how I could help with art related projects.

After several weeks helping in the classroom with various menial tasks, the headteacher asked me into the office to explain how she thought I was starting to look board with the responsibilities involving support work in a primary school and suggested I deliver an art lesson to one of the classes. My eyes must have lit up, revealing my delight at the prospect, as she immediately returned a knowledgeable smile.

The following week, I received a schedule that involved delivering three art lessons that would include every pupil in the school. The first taking place in the morning, before break time, which involved teaching pupils aged five-six. After break, pupils aged seven-eight. And after lunch, the older children aged nine-ten.

Having received no training, I must admit to being extremely nervous prior to my first ever attempt at teaching. My strategy was to ignore all the teachers present and concentrate on giving simple and clear instructions at every stage.

I'd been given a flip chart to which I taped my large A2 paper, introduced myself to the pupils and gave a brief summary of what we would be drawing, a large clear image of two cats sitting on a wall gazing at the moon with their tails entwined (based on the ceramic plate Lynne and I had bought whilst on holiday in Clacton). The image would be relatively simple for the kids to copy and, with colour added, make an impressive picture to take home and impress their friends and family.

I drew the image in short stages, accompanied with clear encouraging instructions and gave plenty of time for the pupils to copy at each stage. Members of staff were surprisingly brilliant and whenever a child appeared to be struggling, they'd intervene, being fully aware of their individual ability and needs. The next stage involved using chalk pastels to colour the composition. Most pupils had never previously used pastels and so it became an exercise in learning new media, as well as drawing.

To my utter surprise and joy the teaching lessons were a tremendous success and thoroughly enjoyed by the pupils, helped immensely by the support of *The Green's* headteacher, who had the foresight to arrange a practical art lesson for all of her pupils by a trained and qualified artist. A couple of weeks later, I thanked her for giving me the opportunity and confidence to teach and said my goodbyes before enrolling onto the *PTLLS (Preparation in Teaching in the Lifelong Learning Sector) Teacher Training Course* at the Sutton Community Academy in Nottinghamshire.

All the students were practising teaching at least three hours each week, a requirement necessary prior to being accepted onto the course. I was teaching weekly art lessons to a small group of adults with learning difficulties. Our class of trainee teachers consisted of about ten individuals from a variety of backgrounds, ages ranging from early twenties to mid-fifties.

To my surprise, they weren't all silver tongued professional academic types that I'd anticipated. Each had their own individual reason for wanting to acquire an adult teaching qualification, such as teaching sixth form students, reform centres and prisons, colleges and adults with special education needs and learning difficulties. My initial interest was to teach *Lifelong Learning courses,* previously referred to as 'Night School'.

A few weeks into our training, during a teatime break, I was enthusiastically showing slides of my *climate change* paintings to my colleagues. John, an elderly student, appeared utterly disinterested with my slides before asking to see my hand, after close examination, he declared how "soft it was— [and had]—obviously seen little physical work."

Initially, I was shocked at his candid abruptness and assumed it was a case of inverted snobbery, I protested vigorously, declaring how hard I'd worked all my life!

John was very tall with strong distinct lines over his weather-beaten face and had a strong Nottingham accent. During an introductory presentation in the classroom, I realised he was training to teach young people who'd been in trouble with the law and wanted to help them develop vocational skills such as bricklaying and plastering, to gain a recognised certificate that would help develop their self-esteem and ultimately, their rehabilitation. And here I was showing off my bright colourful pictures with my subtle, porcelain-like, workshy hand.

I was more intrigued than offended by John's assumption of me being a pompous, privileged academic. His observation was more amusing than offensive. I was impressed with his bluntness and candidness, there was a certain honesty about him that I liked and, further on in the course, we got to know each other more and developed a mutual understanding and respect which involved supporting each other during presentations and the dreaded *micro-teach* which we had to successfully complete to achieve our *PTLLS* qualification.

During this period, I was still exhibiting and selling artwork, which I planned to continue doing whilst teaching. However, it soon became obvious that a teacher's work is never done. Between delivering lessons my time was taken up with planning lessons and marking work, planning presentations, creating timetables and content for courses, responding to emails from admin, attending 'continuous professional development' (CPD) meetings, health and safety meetings and writing essays for my teacher training course.

Teaching is a way of life rather than merely being a job and it soon became clear I wouldn't have time to paint, exhibit work and teach. By now my commitment was firmly with teaching and I'd become part of their community. We were a close-knit team who relied on each other to prevent the wheels from coming off. I'd started teaching adults with learning difficulties and felt responsible for their development, both academically and socially, some had been let down by the establishment in the past, yet trusted me and relied upon my belief in them.

From 2011-2015 I taught art at the *Sutton Community Academy* from beginner to advanced level. The poster is advertising my *Acrylic Course for Beginners*.

SuttonCentreCommunityCollege
A Specialist Business & Enterprise and Arts College

Adult and Community Learning

Acrylic Painting for Beginners
Wednesday 19th September 2012 12.30-2.30pm at Centre Point
Tutor: Mark Cawood

Course Summary
Suitable for beginners wishing to gain experience working with acrylic paints. The atmosphere is relaxed and non-judgemental, allowing students to progress at their own pace. Compositions include landscapes and still-life paintings, created in a variety of styles that are inspired from photographs and 3D objects.

Entry Requirements
No previous experience is necessary, enthusiasm and enjoyment are the most important entry requirements.

How much time will I spend on the course?
2 hours per week, there will be no compulsory homework

How is the course delivered?
The course combines teacher input, including practical demonstrations, and student activity using active learning approaches.

Who is this course suitable for?
The course is suitable for students wishing to explore their potential in painting using acrylic paints, no experience is required.

What materials do I have to provide?
Acrylic paints and brushes of various size, A4 and A3 heavy duty paper.

Is there anything else I need to know about this course?
You will receive regular feedback on your progress and be given opportunities for one-to-one tutorials.
Please turn over for additional information

These courses are provided in partnership with Nottinghamshire County Council.

Funded by
Skills Funding Agency

Nottinghamshire County Council

For further information contact:

Adult Education Office
Sutton Centre Community College
High Pavement
Sutton-in-Ashfield
Notts, NG17 1EE

Telephone: 01623 441310 or 442173

Website: www.suttoncentre.co.uk

Email: admin.adulted@suttoncentre.notts.sch.uk

A couple of years later, I became the tutor for art GCSE and A'level, whilst continuing with short adult learning courses. Showing a page from the 2014 college brochure, containing my teaching programme and a short profile of art student Andrea, who progressed to university after attending several of my *Lifelong Learning* courses.

Art

Art for Beginners

Tues	23/09/14	12.30-14.30	BCB	6 Wks
Tues	23/09/14	18.30-20.30	TBC	6 Wks

Art GCSE

Fri	19/09/14	9.30-14.30	ASCH	36 Wks

Art A Level

Thurs	18/09/14	9.30-14.30	BCB	36 Wks

Drawing for Beginners

Tues	18/11/14	18.30-20.30	TBC	4 Wks

Illustration for Beginners

Tues	18/11/14	12.30-14.30	BCB	4 Wks

Painting and Drawing - Intermediate

Mon	22/09/14	12.30-14.30	ASCH	6 Wks

Andrea started a Drawing and Illustration course at SCA as she hoped it would help with her voluntary work at the John Eastwood Hospice, where she leads a painting class for patients. Andrea then went on to take the Art Advanced class, and with the encouragement of her tutor, Mark, who saw the potential within her, she applied to join a distance learning Degree course in Creative Arts. Andrea says that without the support of Mark she wouldn't have had the confidence to apply to go on the course, which she is very much looking forward to starting.

Beauty

Beauty Skills - Beginners

Fri	26/09/14	9.30-11.30	SCA	6 Wks

Hairdressing

Tues	23/09/14	18.30-20.30	SCA	6 Wks

Look Good - Style and Make up

Fri	21/11/14	11.30-13.30	SCA	4 Wks

Look your Best - Make up / Nails / Beauty

Thurs	25/09/14	18.30-20.30	SCA	6 Wks

Make up - Beginners

Sat	01/11/14	9.00-13.00	SCA	2 Wks
Fri	21/11/14	9.30-11.30	SCA	4 Wks

Nail Art

Mon	22/09/14	18.30-20.30	SCA	6 Wks

Nail Art - Beginners

Wed	24/09/14	18.30-20.30	SCA	6 Wks
Sat	04/10/14	9.00-13.00	SCA	2 Wks

Nail Art for the Festive Season

Mon	17/11/14	18.30-20.30	SCA	4 Wks

Nail Techniques - Beginners

Fri	26/09/14	11.30-13.30	SCA	6 Wks

Party Make up / Nails / Style

Tue	18/11/14	18.30-20.30	SCA	4 Wks

Spray Tanning - Beginners

Tue	23/09/14	18.30-20.30	SCA	6 Wks
Thurs	20/11/14	18.30-20.30	SCA	4 Wks

Waxing - Beginners

Mon	22/09/14	18.30-20.30	SCA	6 Wks

Waxing - Learn the Basics

Wed	19/11/14	18.30-20.30	SCA	4 Wks

Listening to You

We encourage all learners to share their views, concerns and comments with us to ensure that we respond to your needs and requirements. Perhaps you have an idea for a new course? Please let us know by phoning the Adult Education Office on 01623 441310, emailing us at adult.office@suttonacademy.attrust.org.uk, or popping your thoughts into our Suggestion Box, located at our Adult Reception.

For more information visit our website www.suttonacademy.attrust.org.uk or call 01623 441310

It was a privilege teaching students from a wide variety of backgrounds and ages, different cultures, religions, professions, class, colour, disability and gender. I had the pleasure of meeting an extremely diverse group of people that I'd never otherwise have met. Many were retired, disabled or unemployed. Professions included Orthopaedic Surgeons, Detectives, Widows, Heavy Goods Drivers, Psychiatrists, Teachers, Firemen and Nurses.

Many students attended courses as a step towards further education or to help conquer their anxieties or other mental health issues. Others simply wanted to improve their creative talent and required professional direction regarding relevant knowledge, skills and techniques. Some attended primarily for social reasons, perhaps they just needed to break up the monotony of their daily routines.

Students with vastly differing levels of ability, often enrolled onto the same course and, being community orientated, they were all accepted, which is why creating *Individual Learning Plans* were essential prior to any *Lifelong Learning course* commencing. It was equally important to accommodate students' different learning styles, such as visual, audible and kinaesthetic (hands-on), which were also included in my lesson plans.

My lessons virtually always began with a *show and share* section in which each student would show their recent artwork and discuss, with the rest of the class, positives and areas requiring improvement. The class was encouraged to ask questions and offer opinions in a supportive and constructive manner. The exercise served to bond students, improve their subject knowledge and encourage self-esteem and confidence.

When teaching art at the advanced level, I invariably always incorporated particular artists into the lesson plans. Such as Impressionist Mary Cassatt, the only American among the founding members of the Impressionist movement that grew out of late nineteenth century Paris.

Students were assigned to create a rendition of her painting *The Boating Party,* 1893, a beautiful composition containing intricate and expressive brushwork, captivating the intimate bond between mother and child. The practical exercise helped students identify, firsthand, how using thick impasto brushstrokes can be used to create feeling and atmosphere within a painting, often associated with *Impressionism*. Cassatt reportedly said the objective when painting, was to convey women as "subjects, not objects."

David Alfaro Siqueiros, born in 1896, was a Mexican *Social Realist* artist who I often used to introduce students to the concept of narrative art. Siqueiros was admitted to the *San Carlos Academy* at the young age of fifteen.

He spent many years in jail for his political activism, which influenced his art greatly, resulting in many of his paintings depicting suffering during life in prison. His travels to Europe brought him in contact with the artwork of Goya and their themes and images of war in their works are very similar. Siqueiros believed that "art must no longer be the expression of individual satisfaction, but should aim to become a fighting educational art for all."

Examples of his work include *Echo of a Scream,* inspired by his experiences during active combat and his observations of suffering amongst innocent victims of war. *New Democracy* depicts a woman trying to shatter the bonds of oppression and exploitation. And *Cain in the United States*,

1947, is an uncompromising graphic painting conveying the dangers of an ignorant and hostile society.

The political content of his work offered an opportunity for students to debate the pros and cons of his work and whether he successfully conveyed his views. Students were then required to create a rendition of one of his paintings. Such projects frequently involved heated debate, which, as their tutor, I was pleased to witness students develop subject knowledge, confidence and, in some cases, a self-belief that excelled in abundance.

My advanced classes often included *Art déco* artist Tamara de Lempicka, born in Poland in 1898, though spent most of her life as a professional artist in America and Paris. She created highly polished portraits of the aristocracy and stylised paintings of nudes. In contrast with Impressionism,

Lempicka's paintings contained no visible signs of brushstrokes, such as *Young Lady Wearing Gloves,* 1930 and students who undertook the task of creating a rendition of her work were certainly stretched and challenged.

The Art déco movement celebrated contemporary affluence and modern technology such as fast new passenger planes, trains and ships and was most popular from around nineteen-twenty to nineteen-forty. However, its appeal had faded by the end of the Second World War, when the vast majority of people were on rations and couldn't afford to indulge in such affluence.

My *advanced mixed media* course included Chris Ofili's poignant narrative work, particularly *No Woman No Cry*, as an example of how mixed media can be used to convey a powerful statement, opinion or personal heartfelt message.

The *mixed media* course involved much emphasis on experimentation with a variety of media including materials to create texture, such as sand or flour and mixing oil and water-based paints to create a marbling effect. Students would eventually be tasked with creating their own narrative work using knowledge gained during their research and personal experience, experimenting with a variety of materials to complete their own final piece.

During the beginning of an *Illustration* course in 2014, I discussed with my students the possibility of exhibiting their work at a local venue such as a library or council building. We discussed in depth what theme of work would be of interest to the local community and subjects they would be interested in painting for the exhibition.

I'd taught most of the group previously and so we knew each other pretty well, their ages ranged from about thirty to seventy-five and I was aware of their artistic ability and motivation, most had successfully copied Tamara de Lempicka's painting *Young Girl with Gloves* and so I was confident they'd rise to the challenge.

I could see they were immediately interested and as we talked and suggested ideas, the group gradually became more enthralled.

Eventually, we agreed on a theme, students were to produce two paintings each, one conveying an old scene relevant to the local community, Sutton-in-Ashfield (an old coal mining town) and a second conveying the town today.

We would call the exhibition *Old and New* and the following week my students were given a deadline to complete the work after I'd arranged a two-week exhibition at Sutton Library.

Sutton Community Academy

Adult and Community Learning

Sutton - Past and Present

**Artwork Exhibition
At Sutton Library
From Monday 3rd – 17th June 2013**

Illustration students from Sutton Community Academy are holding an exhibition of artwork at Sutton Library from Monday 3rd till 17th June, entitled 'Sutton – Past and Present'. The artwork will convey the local community through portraits and buildings both from the past and present. All exhibited artwork will be for sale within an affordable price range.

The exhibition is being organised and arranged by members of staff from Sutton Community Academy who together with Sutton Library, participated in the World Book Day which served as the initial inspiration for the 'Sutton – Past and Present' exhibition – a showcase of art that will interest both young and elderly members of Sutton community.

In partnership with

Nottinghamshire County Council

Funded by
Skills Funding Agency

For further information contact:

Adult Education Office
Sutton Community Academy
High Pavement
Sutton-in-Ashfield
Notts, NG17 1EE

Telephone: 01623 441310 or 442173

Website: www.suttonacademy.attrust.org.uk

Email: adult.office@suttonacademy.attrust.org.uk

The standard of artwork created during the *Old and New* exhibition project was extremely high and included interesting and thought-provoking narratives such as David's painting depicting wind turbines in the foreground, with gas towers in the distance. There were paintings of miners using their horse to pull heavy loads of coal, a local hospital and other recognisable local buildings and sites.

Liz Barrett, the director at *Sutton Community Academy*, was very supportive of the venture and even submitted her own painting that she'd created especially for the exhibition. An impressive and competently painted acrylic on canvas depicting a well-established local church. My students and I were busy hanging the artwork at Sutton Library when a local reporter turned up, complete with a camera around their neck, *which* resulted in a two-page spread in the local newspaper.

I had a lot of time for Liz, she'd been a tutor at the academy before progressing to a section leader and then director of the college, which I believe enabled her to empathise with tutors and understand their concerns. Despite being extremely busy, she always managed to find time for her staff, including tutors, administration, the caretaker and the students.

She was particularly knowledgeable and supportive concerning courses for students with special needs, which was a large part of my teaching schedule. And was constantly trying to acquire local or national funding for much needed courses that would benefit the community. Unfortunately, during this period, government policy reduced spending every year, particularly adult learning and many of the academy's Lifelong Learning courses became increasingly shorter or were cancelled altogether.

I saw a post on Facebook recently, stating Liz had been awarded a medal at Buckingham Palace for her superlative work within the education sector. All I can say is that she thoroughly deserves such acknowledgement, though increasing grants for education would, in my opinion, be a far more practical gesture of goodwill.

About a year later, I helped arrange a similar exhibition for members of the *Cornwater Club* for the elderly in Nottinghamshire, where I held weekly art sessions for several years. There were several themes for the show, including birds, insects, plants and animals, roughly one for each wall within the venue, this time held at *Mansfield Central Library* where I'd previously delivered many public art demonstrations and classes.

During my time teaching *English Functional Skills* at secure hospitals, I had to be confident each student was fully prepared and capable of passing their exam. All the students were vulnerable and had individual learning needs, a mentally gruelling exam could be exhausting or simply overwhelm such students and, should they fail, destroy their confidence and the possibility of progressing any further within education.

The *English Functional Skills* exams involved a verbal *question-and-answer* section that had to be performed in front of their peers, as well as a comprehensive section involving written tasks. The majority of my students had left school without a single qualification, which had left them lacking in self-confidence and sceptical towards anyone in authority. Consequently, I felt it was of paramount importance to give my students the best possible chance in passing their exams.

My English lessons were often delivered as art lessons with Functional Skills embedded into the content. Emphasis would often be placed on a practical drawing exercise, for example, a complete lesson would be dedicated to learning how to accurately draw a three dimensional looking car, which they were deservedly proud of on completion.

The next lesson involved creating labels to describe parts of their car, which helped develop spelling ability. They would then be guided on constructing sentences to describe the colour, age and make of their car. The final lesson involved writing a paragraph to describe an adventure in their car.

I had a good constructive relationship with my students and very rarely resorted to discipline. I delivered lessons designed to avoid an *us and them* atmosphere and believe my disability helped in this, it made me less imposing or threatening and students frequently offered to help me with physical tasks such as moving tables or other heavy work, which served to help the class bond.

After about six months, many of my students had successfully achieved their English Functional Skills qualification, a recognised national qualification through the teaching provider AIM. As a result, many were extremely delighted with themselves and their confidence, as a self-respecting person, had visibly grown by leaps and bounds.

After my accident there'd always been a rather precarious relationship between my work and my disability and by 2015, I was becoming increasingly unsteady on my legs and began to find it difficult carrying large and heavy props, books and painting materials to and from classrooms, particularly if there was a great distance between the car park or staff room and classroom.

During this time, I had been accepted for a role teaching art in a prison, however the hours were full-time and, consequently due to my deteriorating condition, I felt obliged to decline.

My final two years of teaching mainly involved supply work at three secondary schools in Derbyshire. My first day at Belper High School was quite an eventful experience. I'd arrived quite flustered, having had trouble finding the venue via my satnav that kept insisting I'd arrived at my destination despite my driving on a remote dirt track with nothing visible but large trees and bushes.

I crawled along slowly until I came to a tall stonewall, then a gate and, hey presto, I finally saw the sign for Belper School! I produced my ID at the reception desk and was asked to wait whilst she identified the room in which I would be teaching. Several minutes later, she returned to advise it was room four down the corridor on my left.

I entered the room and saw five children aged roughly between eight and twelve, three of which were accompanied by a personal support worker due to their special needs. Support workers in the classroom can be an invaluable source of additional help for teachers, particularly when there are students with special educational needs.

I introduced myself to the class before noticing there were no lesson plans visible, which I'd been advised would be left on the desk with clear instructions. *Not to worry,* I thought and feeling positive, remembered a lesson I'd recently delivered to a class with special needs at Sutton Community Academy, involving students making a unique and personally coloured flag using the union jack design as a blueprint.

One of the support workers obtained a set of glue sticks and modelling scissors, then brought out a large box from the storeroom, containing lots of coloured paper, fabric and card, some metallic, perfect for our flag making lesson. The lesson progressed well with children obviously enjoying the kinaesthetic process involved with making a flag. Glue, glitter, fabric and card stuck to tables, chairs, clothes and hair and, after much perseverance, the flags were beginning to take shape.

After about fifty minutes there was a knock on the classroom door and the receptionist entered to say, "I've been on the phone to confirm your booking with *Teachers UK* (my agency) and they tell me you're supposed to be teaching at *Belper High School,* NOT *Belper School for Special Needs*."

The unexpected interruption had stopped everyone in their tracks and they turned to me in anticipation for some kind of instruction. I could feel my face turning bright red as I offered an apologetic self-conscious smile before shuffling out of the classroom, feeling utterly embarrassed. After sorting out what had been a massive misunderstanding, eventually I arrived at the correct destination, *Belper High School,* albeit two and a half hours later than had been arranged.

I ended up teaching at *Belper High School* quite regularly and enjoyed the experience. They held unconventional policies, such as teachers and students addressing each other by their first names and didn't have a uniform policy, enabling students to dress how they liked. The relaxed rules worked and I found students to be generally more mature and less rebellious in comparison to other schools where I'd taught.

I recall delivering an *Information Technology* lesson for a *year eight* class (aged between twelve and thirteen) when teaching at a school in Matlock. My brief stated pupils must 'open their *Summer Festival Project* folder and, using *word,* develop their plans for a summer festival—'

I introduced myself and read out their instructions for the lesson. As I turned around to reiterate the instructions on the whiteboard, I became aware of a boy acting silly, he was quite excitable and generally causing a distraction.

I asked the class whether anyone had any queries and made sure all students knew what they had to do before focusing my attention on the silly boy, primarily to make sure he wasn't intent on distracting the other students from their work. His name was Tim and it soon became apparent he was dyslexic when I realised he couldn't spell basic words. I sat down beside him and dictated the correct spelling for words Tim chose for his project. He immediately became focused and began typing onto the keyboard with tremendous enthusiasm once he was receiving appropriate support.

Tim's ideas for his *Summer Festival Project* were impressive, being realistic, practical and considerate, involving parking spaces, toilets for the disabled, food and drink stalls and ticket price reductions for the elderly, "so I can bring my nan."

Tim wasn't receiving an unfair advantage, simply receiving help with spelling due to his dyslexia. All the ideas for the project came from his imagination and inventiveness and I was genuinely impressed.

Tim's dyslexia was absent from my lesson plan notes, however such crucial information should have been highlighted clearly to assist with the supply teacher's teaching strategy, more importantly Tim should have had a teaching assistant, specialising in dyslexia, with him throughout his learning.

Tim was enthusiastic, well-motivated and created a well thought-out plan for a summer festival, all he needed was someone to spell out his choice of words. He obviously appreciated my support and returned the favour by handing in a well thought-out and articulate piece of work at the end of the lesson. He was an intelligent young man who, initially during the lesson, was frustrated by not having one-to-one support.

As a supply teacher, before going home, I would hand all paperwork into reception. On this occasion, I wrote on the lesson notes that "Tim would excel in leaps and bounds, particularly in academic subjects, should he receive one-to-one support from a teaching assistant, preferably someone trained in helping special needs and dyslexia." I am not blaming this particular school for Tim's lack of specialist support.

Unfortunately, virtually all schools across the country are desperately short of teaching assistants due to an acute lack of funding by the present UK government, particularly those trained to assist pupils with special education needs.

On one occasion, at *Belper High School,* I was given the task of teaching a *year eleven* class (aged around fifteen). My lesson plan notes stated the class 'lacked motivation and they generally resented being in school.' The lesson required they write an essay on what they believed were their strong points and talents.

Before any writing commenced I thought a ten-minute chat may help me to familiarise the students' attitude and identify their general academic ability. I was already aware the class had little confidence and so told a story about an old school friend who "had never passed any of his exams when he left school but, after years of hard work and persistence, he developed skills involving carpentry, plastering, fitting electrics and central heating, saved enough to buy a cheap, dilapidated house, renovated it and then earned money renting it out. Now he's a landlord who owns several houses that he rents out, contributing to a lifestyle involving travelling the world for six months of each year".

By the time I'd finished, their ears had pricked up and they appeared visibly interested in my story, offering hope and success to which they could empathise with and aspire to achieve themselves. This was one of those lessons that stood out, I could see how positively they'd responded when treated as people with the potential for success, rather than the constant negative feedback they'd become accustomed to in school, even the lesson plan notes had stated they were 'low achievers'.

The following week when I next visited the school, their resident teacher took me to one side to ask how I'd persuaded her 'low achievers' to do such good work, adding how they usually just heckle supply teachers and generally obstruct the progression of each lesson.

After receiving acknowledgement and a thank you for my contribution in the development of so-called 'low achievers', I felt over the moon—Only teaching could make me feel this intensely alive, only teaching could unleash such joy!

08 Nature's Revenge

During my time teaching (between 2011-18), painting took a back seat due to the responsibilities involved with the profession such as planning courses and sessions, marking students' work and assessing their individual learning styles, attending meetings and delivering the sessions.

However, on the few occasions when I did find time to paint, the composition would invariably consist of an environmentally orientated seascape conveying the increasingly disturbing issue of global climate change. I believe the issue has rarely received the priority it deserves by recent governments. It's as though they're either utterly unaware or simply just don't care about the potential catastrophic destruction of our environment if carbon emissions, that heat up our planet, are not dramatically reduced soon.

It is generally accepted by all reputable scientists internationally, that global climate change is a real and genuine threat to civilisation as we know it, resulting in the extinction to the majority of wildlife including pollinating creatures that will have a detrimental effect on our crops causing mass starvation on a global scale.

Oceans absorb more than ninety percent of heat trapped by the planet due to the increasing concentrations of greenhouse gases in the atmosphere. As the water heats up, its volume expands and causes a rise in sea levels. Warmer oceans will lead to increased rainfall and stronger, more frequent storms.

As the planet gets warmer, melting icebergs also contribute to rising sea levels. Consequently, low-level coastal areas around the world face the continuous threat of flooding, with some areas becoming uninhabitable and may eventually become submerged. Nations such as the Maldives, Barbados and Tuvalu are continuously being flooded by extreme cyclones and meteorologists forecast they're likely to disappear permanently beneath the sea within the next fifty years.

According to *Metro News (online 2020)*, the UK will fare no better with rising sea levels threatening to submerge large areas within the next thirty years, including North Wales, the east coast of England ranging from Sunderland to Norfolk and Camber on the south coast, resulting in the loss of tens of thousands of homes, businesses, farmland, railways and holiday resorts.

Data collected by *UK's Environment Agency* suggest areas of London also risk being submerged, with Greenwich, Fulham and Walthamstow being most vulnerable. London councillors response is rather apathetic, claiming the public should not be alarmed assuring there are plans to 'build walls'.

A few years ago, Lynne and I were house hunting on the south coast and arranged to view a property in Peacehaven near Brighton. The bungalow had impressive kerb appeal with a large well maintained front garden, wide driveway and an array of beautiful plants around the borders. The interior was even more impressive, consisting of large elegant rooms and a superior decor than anything we'd previously viewed.

The middle-aged couple selling the property were both present and I couldn't help noticing how the woman appeared to be unsettled and rather distressed. I then noticed the man who was showing us around, also appeared flustered and was sweating profusely. For a brief moment I wondered whether they'd had a row prior to our arrival. We continued with the tour and, after entering each of the luxurious rooms, grew evermore interested, even a little excited.

I asked to see the rear garden, which was accessible via the kitchen door. As we walked out, I was surprised by the disproportionately small size of the lawn that appeared to be uncomfortably exposed to a cliff face at the end, where fresh cracks and loose soil were visible on the lawn.

Beyond the garden was a rather imposing view of an angry sea, complete with large unforgiving waves crashing relentlessly into the bottom of this vulnerable little garden. Spray from the waves were landing on the lawn and occasionally drops splashed on our clothes, then I felt a cold drop hit my cheek, causing me to shiver involuntarily, but not because it was cold.

The wind howled whilst Lynne constantly pushed her hair back to prevent it from covering her face. I turned to the man and noticed the hair on his balding head was soaking wet with sweat, he ignored the open cliff edge and spray on the lawn, as he gestured we follow him to the side access. Lynne and I looked at each other and simultaneously shrugged our shoulders, it was clear we weren't going to live on the edge of a crumbling cliff face.

I informed the sweating man that we had to leave as we had another viewing to attend, which wasn't true but seemed the best way to make our escape. As I entered the car, I could hear the distressed woman crying from the bungalow. She was sobbing uncontrollably and it suddenly dawned on me how this poor couple were trapped in a beautiful luxurious bungalow, that was literally being devoured by a relentless incoming sea. We began driving off when Lynne asked, "What did you think?"

I replied, "We've just visited paradise in hell."

A selection of Nature's Revenge paintings.

Our climate can be unpredictable and sometimes very erratic, no one can be sure what effect it will have on us from one day to the next. We can be leisurely absorbing vitamin D on a sun-drenched beach whilst, at the very same time, people in another country are dying of thirst and hunger from the very same source.

Norfolk Broads *Oil on canvas. 80 cm x 60 cm*

The Norfolk Broads paintings convey an area of land destined to become the sea as a result of climate change. I could have chosen an alternative title from the many locations vulnerable to becoming submerged, however, I chose the Norfolk Broads as this area has already begun to submerge with land being consumed by the incoming sea. Inspiration for the paintings developed from an article in *The Guardian* by Patrick Barnham in 2008, entitled *Waves of Destruction*. Here is an extract:

The government's environmental body, National England, said that nine miles of sea defences between the Norfolk seaside villages of Eccles and Winterton were unsustainable "beyond the next 20-50 years", creating the possibility of "realigning the coast". What this cold academic language means is wiping part of Norfolk off the map: 600 homes, six villages, five medieval churches, four freshwater Broadland lakes, historic windmills, precious nature reserves and valuable agricultural land would be given up to the rising seas and Britain would have its first climate change refugees.

Defences have been allowed to disappear completely and in less than a decade the sea has marched several hundred metres inland. In 2008, the chief executive of the Environment Agency, Lady Young, responsible for defending Britain's coastline told a recent climate change conference, "I think the Norfolk Broads will go. They will definitely salinate."

Around sixteen million people presently live close to Britain's coastline. Norfolk is one of the first areas to confront what every low-lying community in the country will face in the coming decades. A consequence of global warming exacerbated by the ever-increasing carbon emissions and subsequent rising sea levels, excessive weather conditions and erosion of sea defences.

Norfolk's landscape has dramatically changed in recent years with neat lines of wheat crops ending abruptly at a cliff edge. Such relentless erosion to coastlines is happening so fast that crops planted last autumn to be harvested this summer have already been lost to the sea.

Norfolk Broads in Sunset *Oil on canvas. 80 cm x 60 cm*

Large areas of the Norfolk Broads, Great Yarmouth and Norwich could be submerged underwater by 2050 unless drastic action is taken to halt global warming. According to the journal *Oceans and Coastal Management (online 11/11/2022)* sea levels around the English coast are forecast to rise thirty-five centimetres by 2050 with lowland areas being particularly vulnerable, such as Norfolk, Sunderland, parts of Yorkshire, London and Camber on the south coast.

Relic *Oil on canvas. 80 cm x 60 cm.*

Developed from a photograph I'd taken during a holiday in Spain with the family. When I first saw this sunken boat, I had no camera on me and had to run back to the hotel and acquire film before returning to the scene. The image of this sunken boat was initially used as part of my *Mourning Spring* painting from *The Distance Between Land and Sea* collection. I kept reworking this piece until I was satisfied with the balance between abstraction and reality.

Scarlet Evening in December *Oil on canvas. 80 cm x 60 cm.*

The tsunami was caused by an undersea earthquake. The initial rupture occurred in the Indian Ocean near the west coast of Sumatra, creating a six-hundred mile parting of the Earth's crust that caused powerful shock waves and displaced trillions of tons of rock.

The tsunami waves didn't reach coastlines until several hours after the initial undersea rupture had occurred, unfortunately virtually all of the victims were taken completely by surprise as a result of no earthquake warning systems being in place. Eyewitnesses in Indonesia reported seeing animals fleeing to high ground several minutes prior to the gigantic tsunami waves reaching the coastline. Apparently, hardly any animal bodies were found in the aftermath of the disaster.

I'd been working on this painting when the tragic Indian tsunami occurred on 26 December 2004, which influenced the eventual narrative of the piece. The pose of the woman in the foreground is loosely inspired by Impressionist Frederic

Bazille's painting *The Pink Dress*, 1865. The pictorial content places the individual elements into a field of tension. Originally intended for my earlier *Distance* paintings, I left the piece unfinished for several years before finally returning to the somewhat sombre subject to commemorate such a horrific natural disaster.

Tsunami *Oil on canvas. 80 cm x 60 cm.*

The tsunami's waves travelled across the Indian Ocean at around five-hundred miles per hour. The undersea earthquake caused a shift in the Earth's mass and was powerful enough to change the planet's rotation. The tsunami had an impact on eleven countries reaching three-thousand miles to Africa where people died and properties were destroyed.

Deaths caused by the tsunami reached 227,898. Developed from the painting *Scarlet Evening in December,* the title is self-explanatory and conveys a poignant, intimate moment involving a young woman grieving the death of a loved one lying in the sea.

Blue Horizon *Oil on canvas. 80 cm x 60 cm.*

The composition is simple, yet illustrates perfectly the unique beauty of our living planet. Part of the *Amazon Rainforest* the size of Belgium has disappeared during the past three years and many indigenous people are being forced out of their homes.

For example, the *Yanomami tribe* are dying from diseases brought in by miners who blow up their local habitat with dynamite, resulting in contaminated rivers and subsequent dead fish, birds and other wildlife that are a vital food source for their sustainability. Seventy percent of the global wildlife population has disappeared over the past fifty years, with over a million species now being threatened with extinction. Our planet is beautiful, yet fragile.

Sea of Souls *Oil on canvas. 80 cm x 60 cm.*

I focused on creating a visibly heavy atmosphere by emphasising thick clouds to represent carbon emissions and greenhouse gases that, in reality, are completely invisible and consequently may cause people to hold a false sense of security. The painting successfully conveys a melancholic mood concerning climate change, however the composition risks making the horrific truth appear almost beautiful.

Environmental Meltdown *Oil on canvas. 80 cm x 60 cm.*

The aim was to create a sense of perspective and depth within the painting, to convey the magnitude of rising sea levels globally. The figure in the foreground demands the viewer's attention, placed enigmatically within an eternal entanglement of nature.

Superficially, the figure could be bathing in paradise, however a closer look reveals a darker truth, the water is moving rapidly within a hot climate and appears to contradict the lone tree, looking conspicuous yet sombre without foliage, suggesting we are witnessing a winter heatwave.

In 2022, western parts of America sustained continuous heavy rainfall combined with melting snow around mountains, causing flooding that resulted in catastrophic damage to property and numerous deaths. And related statistics in newspapers such as "The Yellowstone River's water level reached a record high since records began almost one hundred years ago."

Stone Delusion *Oil on canvas. 80 cm x 60 cm.*

During February 2020, the UK sustained devastating flooding from three successive storms—*Clara, Dennis* and *Jorge* resulting in hundreds of thousands of homes being flooded as well as widespread disruption to the surrounding infrastructure. It was the wettest February since UK records began back in 1910, receiving more than twice the annual rainfall.

The painting is based on one of UK's many beautiful stone-age sites with a prophetic message highlighting the potential risk of flooding from the sea, should temperatures keep rising due to excessive carbon emissions, melting icebergs and rising sea levels will cause flooding in vast areas of our mainland.

Iconoclastic Tears *Oil on canvas. 80 cm x 60 cm.*

The candles dominate the composition and look strong positioned just off centre, however a closer look reveals their perpetual vulnerability as they constantly rely upon the supporting hand in order to remain upright and functional. Symbolic of today's society which is ultimately dependent on different sectors working together constructively and in harmony, if we're to preserve our beautiful yet fragile environment and the subsequent rich diversity of life.

For example, trees transform poisonous carbon dioxide into healthy oxygen, yet many companies prefer to cut down trees for wood which produces a short-term profit at the expense of our long-term health. Large areas of rain forests are rapidly disappearing, areas of which contain thousands of species we haven't yet identified and may potentially contain medicinal and therapeutic qualities.

Planting trees may not accumulate as much financial revenue as say an oil rig or coal mine, however ten years down the line the trees will have helped preserve millions of lives including wildlife and the environment, whereas oil and coal will have merely contributed to the decimation of our beautiful fragile planet. When a company dumps toxic waste into a freshwater river, not only do the fish die but the whole food chain is decimated, resulting in many species dying and others becoming susceptible to extinction.

Climate protesters such as *Extinction Rebellion UK* and *Just Stop Oil* feel that constitutional methods such as writing to their MP simply aren't working and consequently are highlighting the global climate crisis through high publicity stunts that are disruptive yet peaceful, such as throwing tomato soup over the glass covering of a Van Gogh painting in a London gallery or gluing themselves to public roads.

Helen Pankhurst wrote an article for *The Guardian (online 2022)*, comparing climate protesters with her grandmother, Sylvia Pankhurst, from the Suffragette movement over a century earlier. Highlighting how both campaigns were and are entirely moral and just, yet reported with outrage by the national media despite their actions being entirely peaceful with the aim of raising public awareness.

Unfortunately, the media are far less outraged when they report people dying as a result of climate change, for example in East Africa, one person dies of climate induced hunger every thirty-six seconds.

The public has become aware of climate change and is generally concerned with government apathy towards scientific research, whose collective conclusion stresses the importance of carbon emissions being dramatically reduced to prevent our planet from overheating, resulting in an environmental disaster on a global scale.

09 Period of Transition

After eighteen months working as a supply teacher in secondary schools every Monday to Thursday, delivering art classes at an elderly persons club on Fridays and driving up to Durham over the weekend to refurbish an old property we'd recently bought. The thought of retirement sounded appealing. Supply teaching had become increasingly difficult concerning access to several of the schools that were surrounded by uneven ground, particularly during the winter in icy and wet conditions.

On one occasion, when it was pouring down with rain, I arrived at the school car park and slipped to the ground as I stepped out from my car and spent the rest of the day teaching in a wet and muddy shirt.

On another occasion, whilst taking a break in the staff room, I was handed a pile of heavy reference books needed for a forthcoming science lesson and found myself balancing them with one hand, somewhat precariously, as I slowly progressed up a flight of stairs whilst trying my best to avoid over energetic teenage kids rushing to their next lesson.

I enjoyed supply teaching but the hours were erratic and the pay wasn't particularly good either. It was time to consider an occupation that was less physically demanding. Lynne and I had discussed the possibility of fostering on several occasions over the years, which we felt would be an ideal joint venture involving Lynne's natural warmth and love for kids, combined with my experience of teaching students with special needs and behavioural issues, developed during my time teaching at secure hospitals where I gained experience liaising with occupational therapists, mental health nurses and care workers.

Our boys had both left home and Lynne appeared to be at a loose end. After we moved from Essex to Derbyshire, she'd drifted apart from her family and I feared she'd become unmotivated and a little isolated. I believed fostering would be a perfect opportunity, not just for her, but for us both to contribute positively within the community, liaise with outside agencies and gain a sense of achievement helping young vulnerable children gain a chance to rebuild their broken lives through, love, support and patience.

On a practical level, we had a large home with two empty bedrooms, we could both drive and had plenty of spare time, relevant skills, commitment and experience of bringing up our two great sons, one with Asperger's Syndrome whose subsequent mental health issues had led to excessive drinking.

During the Easter break in 2018, I informed my teaching agency that I'd be retiring at the end of the summer term. A new career and way of life was an exciting prospect for us both and Lynne began contacting several fostering agencies.

Our eldest son James was thirty and had his own flat but stayed with us during most weekdays on condition he refrained from drinking, due to the negative effects the alcohol caused. When sober, he is an intelligent, well-behaved and likeable young man with a passion for aeroplanes who loves attending airshows with his cine camera, particularly during the summer months.

James' mental health had dramatically deteriorated when he began binge drinking about six years earlier. The time I first realised just how serious his drinking problem had become, I was asleep in bed whilst gradually awakening to a loud desperate scream followed by a thud, then another scream followed by a thud and so on.

This pattern kept repeating until I finally got out from my bed to investigate the noise and was horrified to see James at the bottom of our drive, very drunk, continuously smashing the bonnet of his car with a stick.

Police turned up and after a period of questioning charged him with drink driving. This was his first of many appearances at court involving excessive drinking that eventually led to him receiving a ten year driving ban. Such consequences prevented him from attending his beloved airshows and his depression, combined with heavy drinking, led him to further problems with the law, particularly after he began driving to airshows whilst banned.

Initially, police were supportive however, after his behaviour gradually worsened, police attitude changed from tolerance to contempt and eventually hostility.

On a cold winter's evening in February 2016, I was in the middle of preparing a practical lesson for my elderly students' Friday art class. The doorbell rang and Lynne answered, only to be greeted by a smallish man shouting aggressively into Lynne's face.

By the time I arrived at the front door, the aggressive man had his foot planted firmly inside our hallway, thus preventing Lynne from shutting the door. He was accompanied by a young female and both were loosely dressed in police uniforms, which I assumed they'd acquired from a fancy dress shop. I picked up our landline phone and threatened to call the police, which appeared to deter them sufficiently enough to walk back to their vehicle parked in the road, from where they drove off.

The following day, Lynne and I visited the local police station to ascertain whether the hostile visit by two sinister clown-like characters, claiming to be police officers, had indeed been genuine. The sergeant looked through his files and after a couple of minutes confirmed a visit to our premises had been recorded by one of his officers, we subsequently filed a complaint.

In response, after completing several official forms of complaint, it appeared local officers had closed ranks in a demonstration of loyalty to their colleagues and, following a *freedom of information* request, we discovered false reports and statements were made in what appears to have been a sinister attempt to discredit Lynne's character as a credible witness.

Eventually, we referred evidence of misconduct and corruption to our local MP, who acted as mediator between the two parties. The dispute became a bitter affair and continued for over two and a half years and ultimately had a catastrophic effect on Lynne's mental health.

Three months after I'd retired from teaching, in October 2018, Lynne came home, after dropping James off at his flat and began pacing around the house convinced a plain clothed officer had been following her home. The following day we were in the library and Lynne started having a panic attack, believing members of the public, sitting at a computer or reading a book, were plain clothed officers *out to get her*.

I persuaded Lynne to see her GP on several occasions and eventually she was diagnosed as suffering from paranoid psychosis.

Initially, I felt betrayed. Betrayed by the police for their relentless attack on Lynne's character in a bid to defend a corrupt colleague. Betrayed by family members whose behaviour I felt contributed, albeit indirectly, to Lynne's breakdown. I even felt betrayed by foster agencies, who'd refused our applications on the grounds that foster carers who suffer from psychosis are not considered suitable to look after vulnerable children.

Consequently, all our aspirations involving a dream job of fostering had been smashed into tiny pieces. I felt utterly defeated and could see no future.

Family and friends were trying their best to help Lynne and suggested just about every option possible as a path to recovery. Some were saying *don't take medication* whilst others were saying *take alternative medication*. Some were adamant Lynne received treatment in hospital, whereas others were opposed to such a plan. Quite frankly, it felt as if there were simply too many cooks in the kitchen and what was once a very close-knit family had now irreversibly fragmented. James retreated to his flat, though remained in touch by phone.

After some time, I began to feel sorry for him, as it was obvious he felt a deep sense of guilt concerning Lynne's breakdown, though no one had really noticed at the time, nor blamed James.

If anyone *is* at fault, I believe it lies with today's uncaring society and the relevant institutions that are supposed to protect and support people with mental health issues who, however, choose to ridicule, even criminalise such vulnerable individuals.

The vast majority of people with mental health issues would undoubtedly contribute more positively within society and particularly within the community, with provisions put in place to support their integration both socially and professionally, involving appropriate support and direction which however, could only materialise with vastly improved resources and staff.

Our younger son Christopher applied to join the navy amidst all the chaos and, after an initial culture shock, settled in well. He'll undoubtedly be witnessing some mind-blowing sunsets during voyages across the sea.

He's always had a good work ethic ever since he left school and has tried his hand at a variety of jobs including catering in fast food, welding, care work and retired from being a Heavy Goods driver to finally take the plunge into seafaring, offering a sense of adventure and degree of job satisfaction. It's great to see Lynne's eyes light up when he visits during leave, which always serves as a great excuse to go out for a slap-up meal and enjoy a few drinks.

I found it difficult trying to articulate rationally, irrational behaviour. Everyone simply couldn't understand what was going on and it was unbearable when trying to explain the consequences of a loved one who was experiencing a catastrophic mental breakdown and how it throws all family dynamics into chaos.

Sometimes a relative or friend would try saying something helpful, which, however, merely confirmed their utter lack of understanding. Their ignorance would merely irritate and left me wondering whether they really cared. Did they feel superior, having no apparent signs of mental health issues? Did they think we were to blame?

I wondered and started to dread visits. The weather would invariably be the choice of discussion, merely to kill any unsettling silence and the whole experience was a complete charade. To keep myself from going mad, I devised a game inside my head, which involved contemplating what mental health problems they were hiding behind their supercilious exterior. Nothing of any relevance was ever said and I became good at small talk whilst biting my lip.

Health is the greatest gift, contentment the greatest wealth, faithfulness the best relationship.—Buddha

I was fifty-five, Lynne and I had been together for over thirty years. We had two lovely sons and she was the most important thing in my life, *no*t fostering. Lynne had been by my side every day when I was in hospital following my dreadful motorcycle accident twenty-eight years ago and so it was only fair I helped during her hour of need. Alas, the long and laborious process of recovery began, which involved ensuring medication was taken, maintaining hygiene, encouraging eating and taking liquid and later, providing meals, public days out and keeping her GP up to date with Lynne's progress.

Lynne had lost her appetite completely and became disturbingly underweight. I remember the first time she ate a proper meal; it was half a tin of beans and a round of buttered toast. She may have only eaten one spoonful of beans and half a round of the toast, but it was a major breakthrough and I was deliriously happy. It was a milestone in Lynne's recovery and represented a pinhole of light at the end of a deep, dark tunnel.

Ironically, Lynne's breakdown brought us closer together, we were on the same journey—if she recovered from this nightmare then we both recovered from the nightmare. Little by little, one step at a time, her health improved and we decided to lay the past to rest and move to a new home in a new area. Eventually, after viewing over thirty properties, we found a beautiful three bed bungalow in Northeast Lincolnshire, not far from the sea.

Lynne had regained the weight lost due to illness and showed no signs of a relapse. We were happy and it was great to see her chatting and laughing with neighbours whilst busy gardening and so we accepted an invitation to attend a three day training course in preparation for fostering. The course was held at a hotel in the beautiful Nottinghamshire countryside.

During lunchtime, extravagant three course meals were offered which, I'm sure, the foster care lecturers used as an opportunity to analyse our culinary and social skills at the dining table. The two lecturers delivering the course had previously served as foster carers and helped create a relaxed atmosphere, telling jokes and smiling regularly.

During the first day, Lynne was quiet and content listening to other trainee foster carers contribute to discussions which largely focused on safeguarding issues, procedures and how to resolve potential problems.

On the second and third days, Lynne was putting her hand up and articulating answers to complex questions concerning appropriate action required during emergencies and other relevant scenarios. She explained in tremendous detail what a foster carer must do if a child went missing.

Everyone in the room was visibly impressed with Lynne's plan of action for children, who became unusually quiet or appeared to be intoxicated. She knew what immediate steps to take, who and when to contact various organisations and, most importantly, to remain calm and composed, which would have a beneficial effect on the child.

The lecturers were obviously impressed with her compassion, knowledge and enthusiasm and on the final day offered Lynne and I the opportunity to foster with them and we were each handed a certificate for successfully completing the course. It was Lynne's first certificate of achievement since leaving school forty years earlier and I was immensely proud of her.

Unfortunately, after a routine medical required by foster agencies, results disclosed Lynne had been prescribed medication for psychosis and the fostering agency subsequently dropped us like a hot potato.

Lynne and I had been busy decorating our new home in Lincolnshire. It was a cold and wet morning in February 2022, we were huddled together in the smallest room whilst the plasterer was busy skimming the ceilings when I asked Lynne if she'd like to get married, to which she responded "are you sure you're not acting on impulse?"

There was a satirical element to her response, as we'd originally got engaged thirty-four years earlier but had never got around to tying the knot. Now, just seemed to be the right time, perfectly right.

It was eight thirty-five on a bright sunny morning in June, with less than one hour to go before we were due to get married at Cleethorpes register office. As I approached the car I noticed a massive truck had parked across our driveway with a man operating a crane dropping six foot bundles of fencing and concrete posts onto our garden lawn.

I shouted, "what are you doing?"

He replied, "It's the fence you ordered."

We had ordered a fence, however it was due to be installed the following day. I told the driver we had a very important appointment and he replied, "No problem, I'll only be a few minutes."

By this time, we were pacing up and down and walking in circles with one eye constantly on the time. Then, just as we thought he'd finished, things took a terrible turn for the worse when he said, "Sorry mate, I've just put the wrong posts down. Don't worry, it won't take too long to change them over."

"Oh god no!" I said to myself, "all our contingency time has run out," trying desperately to keep calm. I sat in the car and watched the inept, useless driver fumble with the crane's controls as he proceeded with the laboriously slow process of swapping over our posts.

Then, our neighbour, Linda, came running towards me. I lowered the window. "What's going on?" she asked.

"We're supposed to be getting married in half an hour but we're trapped," and gestured at the massive truck blocking our way.

Linda took one look then declared, "You must go now, drive over my lawn."

I immediately started up the engine and thanked her as the car bounced along her front lawn, I drove swiftly, but carefully, so as to avoid flattening her beautiful rhododendrons, then skilfully weaved past a tree trunk stump I hadn't previously noticed was there. Linda waved goodbye, as did the driver shouting, "Congratulations."

We arrived about ten minutes late, but once I'd paid the outstanding reception fee with my card, the wedding went ahead without any further hick-ups.

After all the formalities were completed and we were finally allowed out of the town hall, we drove to the boating lake nearby. It was a beautiful hot summer's day and we decided to take a romantic trip to the lake by pedalo. Lynne was nervous climbing into the seat and needed a helping hand from the man organising the boat rides. I followed and soon we were off on our first joint adventure as a married couple.

Cleethorpes boating lake is a beautiful, tranquil place full of semi-wild birds, who've become accustomed to being fed by human visitors. We peddled to the end and were navigating around a small island which had an established old tree on the edge with large roots twisting into the surrounding water.

Suddenly, there was an incredibly loud scraping noise coming from the bottom of our pedalo, Lynne and I screamed as we looked at each other for help. The boat came to an abrupt halt, apparently stuck on a massive root from the tree. It took a few seconds for our unfortunate predicament to sink in. Lynne declared, "We are stranded on a boat in the middle of a lake," her tone was of resignation rather than panic.

I replied, "If we wave our arms and shout for help loudly enough, perhaps someone will come to our assistance," trying to offer a degree of optimism.

Lynne looked at me and then rolled her eyes, feeling even more resigned. We could see people walking around the lake, about a hundred yards from our position. I began to shout for help whilst Lynne waved her arms frantically. I'm sure people could hear and see us but, after looking our way, they'd continue walking as if we weren't there. By now we felt completely stupid and decided a new plan was desperately needed.

The situation was compounded by Lynne's deep fear of water and inability to swim. After about half an hour or so, it was decided I'd have to swim to land for help. I leapt off the boat, plunged feet first and suddenly hit the bottom with a hard thud, "Bloody hell!" I cried. "The lake is just a few inches deep!"

Somewhat relieved, I walked the hundred yard stretch to the edge whilst doing my best to look dignified, which was difficult, as people miraculously started to notice our presence. I eventually reached the side, climbed up onto the pathway and continued around the lake until I reached the man standing beside his docked pedalos, to explain our unfortunate predicament. The man was very understanding and told us a similar accident had occurred just a few days earlier.

The summer of 2022 had been the hottest in the UK since records had begun and, during our honeymoon pedalo ride, we were in the middle of a long and relentless heatwave, suffering drought conditions that hadn't seen rain for over a month, consequently the depth of the lake had reduced by over two feet, which led to our pedalo running aground.

After surviving our titanic voyage, it was time for a well-earned drink in the local beer garden.

10 Hello Old Friend

As mentioned earlier in chapter one, I began drawing pictures at a very young age as a necessary means of communication to compensate for my lack of ability in reading and writing. And again, after a life-changing motorcycle accident, I returned to my trusted *old friend*, creating images that served as a source of therapy for my rehabilitation and eventually became the key for opening doors to new and brighter horizons.

The global COVID pandemic resulted in stringent lockdown rules in which everybody's lifestyle was turned on its head, involving schools, shopping centres, offices and factories all closing down rather abruptly and without the necessary provisions put in place. Our infrastructure had stopped functioning, resulting in trains, trucks, traffic and aeroplanes remaining dormant in their respective stations, garages and hangars.

Key workers received a well-orchestrated clap from members of the public every Thursday evening for their selfless dedication to keeping the country afloat during such turmoil. Mental health issues became a national crisis, thousands of people fell victim to the deadly disease on a daily basis and family and friends were prevented from visiting loved ones at funerals, hospitals and care homes.

Yet, paradoxically, I have fond memories of this period, particularly when I recall how fresh and clean the air had become, no doubt a consequence of the dramatic reduction of man-made pollution. Wildlife flourished and became more emboldened, with birds singing louder and clearer than I'd ever previously heard. News reports highlighted how wildlife was reclaiming nature with footage showing herds of deer, stags, goats and sheep entering villages and towns from the surrounding countryside.

I felt optimistic and believed man would realise their grave mistake concerning pollution and its relentless destruction of our beautiful fragile and unique planet and consequently life after the pandemic would become cleaner and greener, with a new and more informed environmentally conscious world and its respective governments.

During the lockdowns, I had plenty of unexpected additional time on my hands and began reading, including several books covering the *American Frontier Wars* during the eighteenth-and-nineteenth-centuries, that involved greed, genocide and broken treaties against the indigenous people. Which concluded with the annihilation of a culture that had lived for thousands of years in perfect harmony, both spiritually and materially, with mother nature and her environment.

The literature described some very sad individual stories involving indigenous people being forced to resettle in reservations hundreds of miles from their natural homeland, where survivors were obliged to convert to western ways, including learning to speak a new language, start practising an alien religion and adapt to a completely different culture and its lifestyle.

For example, a dormitory became their wigwam and metal coins, rather than their trusted bow and arrow, were needed to acquire food and clothing. Thousands of indigenous people died of diseases that had predominantly originated from European settlers to which their bodies had no immune system.

I was outraged and felt compelled to make a visual statement and despite stringent anti-socialising lockdown restrictions during 2020, I could turn to my *old friend,* which culminated in a series of collages. Initial ideas involved simple compositions showing indigenous people living under duress in their new alien environment, including being forced to wear western garments and even the distinctive soldier's blue uniform.

After creating several rough concept pieces, I developed a series of eight collages involving different versions of a specific composition depicting two figures embracing and, being quite pleased with the results, I decided to hang one in our hallway.

Lynne happened to walk by and I asked her opinion. She spent a minute or so looking closely at the collage, before declaring the image appeared to represent a couple in love rather than my intended narrative involving conflict. I admit to being taken aback by her response, having anticipated a more standard analysis such as 'it's alright' or something similar. Though I realised she probably was right, in that images *do* have the potential to convey contradictory messages simultaneously.

Lynne's brief appraisal helped me name the series of A4 size collages which I now affectionately refer to as my *Ambivalent Lemons* (2020-21), due to their message being open to interpretation, whilst containing a somewhat bitter after-taste.

The Ambivalent Lemons:

You cannot wake a person who is pretending to be asleep—Navago.

And so, it appears an image can mean something entirely different from one person to the next, depending on one's individual perspective. Which reminds me of a visit to *The Tate Liverpool Gallery* with my old school friend Ian, who was now an art teacher, where I noticed a somewhat nonsensical abstract piece of art displayed on the wall. I asked, "What does it mean?"

Ian smiled and replied knowledgeably, "Whatever you want it to mean."

I smiled back pretending to be just as knowledgeable, but inside I was thinking, "What kind of answer is that? I would have thought an art teacher could have offered a more meaningful explanation!"

The *Ambivalent Lemon* collages were made from a variety of materials including card, felt and soft leather. The indigenous people were given a headdress using budgerigar feathers and serve as a tribute in memory of our beloved pet budgerigar *Bubble*, who never stopped chatting and singing, was full of fun, mischief, energy and dearly loved by all the family.

Bubble was the leader and we were his flock. He'd always been strong willed and rather stubborn and would dictate when it was time for play and time for bed. He only ever allowed us to watch TV if he didn't feel like singing. Unfortunately, Bubble sustained a serious injury after flying directly into our living room cabinet. Eventually, the injury caught up with him and he passed away in my arms as I gently sang his favourite song, *Yellow Submarine*.

Being a prominent member of the family, we decided to give him a respectful sendoff in the back garden. All the family were present and the mood was solemn. Bubble had been carefully placed in an old shoe box and laid to rest over burning-hot coal on the barbecue. I read some words of sympathy as we all stood with our heads down.

Unfortunately, the flames had little effect and his body refused to disintegrate. The ceremony was momentarily postponed whilst more coal was added and defiantly, whilst the flames turned to cinders, his body remained completely intact. More coal and paraffin were hastily added and still the shape of our beloved Bubble refused to disappear. Even in death, his stubborn nature had shone through. Characteristically, he'd won the battle of wills and we all retired back into the house, pretending such a farce hadn't occurred.

Post-pandemic Art

The main reason I created artwork during the pandemic was to reduce boredom, which usually involved collages developed from limited materials available at the time due to lockdown restrictions and all of the shops being closed.

Post-pandemic, I've concentrated on work conveying contemporary social issues such as the Bird Flu virus and global mental health crisis, consequently my COVID creations have been consigned to the loft.

However, the millions of artefacts created globally during the pandemic, I believe will gradually become desirable by collectors wanting commemorative items in memory of the period. Similar to trench art today, created by soldiers during previous wars that have become highly sought after.

I have read many books by artists over the years, particularly during the pandemic when we had a lot more time to spare, and found they tend to possess similar characteristics and mannerisms, for example I'm left with the impression they're genuinely trying to discover the meaning of life through their art.

I'm motivated from a different perspective involving visual communication that maintains a relationship with reality. For example I have no reservations integrating images with text to convey an opinion, message or statement.

However, there are occasions when art simply refuses to conform with reality or rational thinking, rather like trying to tame a wild animal. Art should develop from realism as opposed to being subject to realism. True and authentic art is boundless and can develop beyond the object, beyond objective reality and its actual configurations.

Art outlives its contemporary moral and ethical perceptions and should not necessarily be created to conform with fashionable ideas of the time. Editing original art to appease contemporary social values merely detracts from the artwork's authenticity, resulting in a Frankenstein-like alternative.

For example, one of The Beatles iconic album covers became a victim to such censorship, highlighted by BBC News back in 2003 who stated: "United States poster companies have airbrushed the classic Beatles *Abbey Road* album cover to remove a cigarette from Paul McCartney's hand." Probably removed to prevent impressionable young fans from taking up the unhealthy habit.

During their heyday in the sixties, The Beatles found themselves subject to censorship by various broadcasters including the BBC, who banned the track *A Day In the Life* due to the lyrics "I'd love to turn you on," that were perceived to be advocating drug use. Which only served to give the track additional credibility amongst the ever increasingly popular *anti-establishment* movement and sales suddenly ascended through the roof.

One of my favourite films *Saturday Night and Sunday Morning*, 1960, was a prelude to the *kitchen-sink* genre, portraying life in a working-class Derbyshire town during the late fifties and documents rather than judges sensitive social issues such as adultery and abortion, with characters constantly puffing away on their cigarettes which is what people did during this era.

However, if such scenes were edited out, the film would undoubtedly lose all credibility as a hard-hitting portrayal of social realism. It is important that people are empowered with information, rather than *protecting* them from true historic facts and events, even those we find difficult to confront. Once you start compromising art, moral values become jeopardised.

Sometimes art conveys through emotion rather than logical rationalism and potentially reaches a more dark and chaotic inner reality. Rene Magritte's painting *Pleasure,* 1927, depicts a young girl devouring a bird, thus reducing the human species to its lowest common denominator by asking whether we're little more than blood thirsty flesh eating creatures?

Magritte's image had an intoxicating impact on me and was a major source of inspiration for my painting *Squashed Pig (see chapter 4)*. I believe it is equally legitimate for a painting to ask a question, as it is to make a statement, as sometimes the objective can be to merely prod the brain into a reaction.

For example, *Squashed Pig* doesn't simply advocate animal welfare, but also asks questions on morality and whether we need to or indeed should, breed intelligent and sensitive animals who often endure a horrendous and uncaring existence inside a confined cage, only to be butchered for the self-serving satisfaction of ending up on our dinner plate.

My recent artwork involves a series of *crisis projects,* focusing on the current international mental health crisis, largely due to natural and man-made catastrophes such as the aftermath of the pandemic. The recent rise in conflict and intense tension between nations and the subsequent *us and them* ethos conveyed on social media, television and inside our newspapers, frequently showing appalling images of civilian casualties that never fail to disgust.

Closer to home we see 'the cost-of-living crisis', involving dramatically rising food and energy prices resulting in mass poverty and new phrases have developed such as *the working poor* and *food-banks* now present in virtually every town across the UK, serving as a last resort in preventing the vulnerable and thousands of working families from going hungry, including many low paid key workers such as nurses, firemen and teachers whilst, in total contrast, directors and shareholders are receiving all-time record profits.

Such orchestrated economic chaos, together with global warming and the pandemic, has resulted in a devastating international mental health epidemic that health services around the world are unable to contain.

Having created many paintings and orchestrated several exhibitions focusing on climate change, I remain concerned with the ongoing climate crisis compounded by public apathy and governments reluctance to invest in green energy in order to reduce high levels of carbon emissions that are rapidly destroying our beautiful planet, predominantly as a result of money. Wind turbines and solar farms may be environmentally friendly, unfortunately however, they don't help oil tycoons become billionaires.

My post-pandemic *crisis projects* involve a variety of media, including relief sculptures, one made using papier mâché and another with casting plaster, a digitally enhanced quadriptych and several collages that aren't yet finished. Here's a preview:

Survivor—As a student, I'd always enjoyed learning about different cultures, particularly *Islamic* and *Egyptian Art*. I was keen to learn about the materials they used and unique style to create calligraphy, ceramics, collages, statues and impressive architecture such as the amazing pyramids.

When designing art courses, as a tutor, I'd invariably include subjects such as *African Art,* culminating in students researching relevant work to design and create their own personal headdress or face mask. The *Chinese New Year* also gave students the opportunity to experiment with a variety of media and get their hands dirty to create large and impressive figurative designs, often involving a tiger, rabbit, snake or a dragon. Such projects were not only culturally informative but also a lot of fun.

I have never personally attempted to create my own face mask, however from relevant lesson plans I developed several concept pieces, that metamorphosed into a living humanoid brick wall to convey the repercussions and consequences involved with surviving a pandemic, culminating in **Survivor**, 2022, made from papier mâché on wood, 70 cm x 50 cm. The work highlights how millions of people are reported to have COVID-19 symptoms many months after they caught the disease, now referred to as *long-covid*.

The UK government introduced emergency laws during lockdown that involved refusing hospital patients and care home residents from receiving visits from loved ones, often resulting in desperately sick people feeling isolated and alone, without loved ones by their side during their final hours. Survivors and family members of such a heartless and cruel law will undoubtedly be suffering from the mental repercussions involving post-traumatic stress.

A being with no relationships is one with no reality.
A non-objective being is an unreal nonsensical thing.
A product of mere thought, merely exists in the mind.
A creature of abstraction cannot be understood.

The Pandemic Sculptures, 2022.

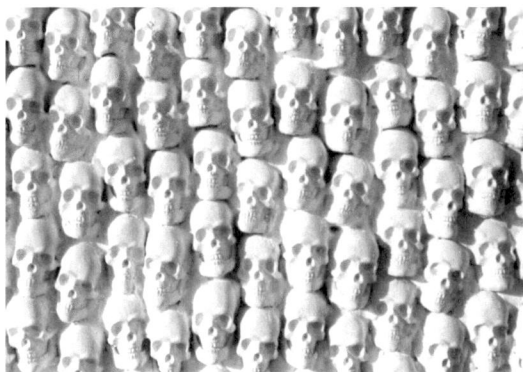

The triptych consists of three relief sculptures, each 40 cm x 30 cm, depicting hundreds of dehumanised human faces in three stages of the pandemic: before, during and after. Made with casting plaster on wood and painted off-white to convey remembrance in the form of a headstone.

Designed to illustrate the devastating effect of a global pandemic and how governments and their countries were utterly unprepared for the devastation, desperation and tragedy that led to millions of premature deaths. The United Nations department of economic and social affairs have estimated 14.9 million excess deaths associated with the COVID-19 pandemic occurred during 2020 and 2021.

The pandemic highlighted how health services around the world were desperately inadequate, had little resources and were dramatically understaffed for dealing with a pandemic. The UK's policy of placing Covid-positive patients into care homes, drew attention to the government's ignorance concerning the disease and resulted in tens of thousands of avoidable deaths.

In the world of art and reality, there is no such thing as an object in itself, because the object is a creation of the subject. *The Pandemic Sculptures* commiserate the dead, whereas *Survivor* commiserates the living. Both convey authentic and highly personal human drama and represent a feeling of bitterness, abandonment and turmoil held by millions globally today.

Savage Hallucination, 2024.

Is a four-piece storyboard initially designed to highlight the devastating effects of drugs and the disturbing consequences of mental health. On reflection, I've become more aware that each and everyone's experience of a mental health crisis is highly personal to their own individual trauma. Consequently, I'm reluctant to attribute the *Savage Hallucination* storyboard to any specific form of mental health crisis, which is generally caused by factors beyond our control.

Whether it be drug or family related, social or health related, the effects of war or a natural disaster such as an earthquake or tsunami or a global pandemic during a severe economic recession. The intense mental stresses involved are all-consuming and need to be addressed on an individual basis by caring and supportive professional bodies.

The quadriptych images were developed from an acrylic/watercolour portrait I'd painted from a photograph of a colleague taken during my time teaching. The digital images convey, in four stages, the gradual deterioration of someone suffering from a personal mental health crisis. In light of the images being digitally enhanced, there's no original copy and when completed, they'll probably be released as limited edition prints.

Commodity Collages consist of a footballer kicking monetary currency in the form of a coin, symbolic of top-flight footballers earning an average weekly wage in excess of £250,000.

Football is an influential sport around the world and therefore has a responsibility to promote diversity, inclusion and equal rights. It is uplifting seeing teams take the knee before a match in support of the campaign *Black Lives Matter*. And I'm constantly impressed with football teams consisting of players from various backgrounds, cultures and continents, working closely together through skill and determination to achieve their goal, often reminiscent of a symphony orchestra performing an inspirational tune. If only the rest of the world could follow their lead.

Unfortunately, there are constant reports of so-called fans who display antisocial behaviour and appear to have little regard for the community, which however, I believe reflects on social problems within their respective society as much as being a football related problem, often relating to poor education and a lack of social funding and resources for public services within the community.

For example, youth clubs give teenagers an opportunity to develop friendships and pursue interests and hobbies in a group environment. Unfortunately, hundreds of such clubs have been closed in the UK during recent years due to a lack of funding.

Top-flight footballers have become a valuable commodity in recent years, the majority of which have risen from working-class backgrounds and to earn such a fortune can only be described as a dream come true.

In contrast, such dreams are less accessible for girls, with less than fifty percent of schools in the UK offering an equal opportunity to play football. Although the government has promised to introduce legislation that will give equal rights regardless of gender, for pupils to participate in football lessons as part of the school curriculum. It will be interesting to see whether such promises materialise.

The *Commodity Collages* remain under development, for example I'm considering adding a rainbow armband to the football figures or some other gesture in support of inclusion, and I'm still searching for a million pound coin that would symbolise the ball perfectly.

Summary

I have seen thousands of benign, mundane paintings that, admittedly, were executed perfectly well and are technically accurate, yet they're instantly forgettable. Many hotel and restaurant chains purposely display neutral art in the form of passive landscapes or nonsensical abstracts in order to avoid advocating any opinion and risk upsetting their customers. Such work conveys no point of view or statement, for its purpose is purely decorative and it is designed to exist in the background.

In contrast, my artwork and the artists I have discussed in this book possess one unifying element, their images are uncompromisingly thought-provoking and consequently demand the viewer's undivided attention, which serves to deliver the narrative of their message clearly and unconditionally. Their images have something of relevance to say, often profound, and are portrayed from a unique and alternative perspective.

When creating a piece of work, I feel privileged to be standing on the shoulder of giants who have introduced the world to new ways of seeing, often through innovative and revolutionary art movements such as the *Impressionists*, *Cubists* and *Surrealists*, to name but a few. Such creative innovation and wisdom are a tremendous source of guidance and inspiration to create new and diverse work.

Particularly, in my case, during the initial planning stage, when a sprinkle of magic is required to develop a concept or idea for my visual commentary on contemporary social and environmental pieces.

For example, Roger Dean's twisted trees are used to create a haunting atmosphere for my painting *Mourning Spring (chapter 5)*. Another oil painting *Rock Guitar (chapter 5)* would never have materialised as a piece of rock in harmony with nature, without the inspiration of Dame Barbara Hepworth's innovative sculptures.

The *Tsunami* painting utilises Impressionist brush strokes to create immediacy and drama within the waves and turbulent sky *(chapter 8)*. And Chris Ofili's experimentation with different media to articulate a sensitive and poignant message inspired me far more than my lecturers during my time at university and influenced much of the experimental work present in the *Food for Thought* project *(chapter 4)*.

Images are immensely powerful, they can be erratic, moral or immoral, good or bad and what they say can have a massive and immediate impact on the viewer, far more so than any written word. You don't have to agree with an image for it to possess influence or even intoxicate your thoughts, conforming is often not the objective.

The image conveys itself without compromise or concession, it is what it is and always will be regardless of any critic's assessment, whether contemporary or historic. An artist can offer an interpretation of their work, but ultimately, the painting will have the final say. Describing a piece of art is comparable to describing the distance between land and sea.

Art should not merely exist as something valuable or new but seek to communicate an idea, a feeling or view, preferably from an original perspective. My latest artwork derives from a personal perspective containing an intimacy not present in previous work, focusing on sensitive issues concerning mental health rather than shouting at the world with moral and political messages. Although I'm fully aware the viewer may perceive the work completely differently.

During the past couple of years I've signed up with several online galleries including *Art-Pal, Fine-Art-America* and *Folksy* where I'm presently showcasing and selling work, and commenced exhibiting in galleries made of bricks and mortar for the first time in over ten years.

I've finally developed my own website, after much contemplation, designed to showcase new visual themes and convey associated ideas with interested parties, an experience that evokes feelings of trepidation and excitement not too dissimilar to that of an explorer about to embark on a new adventure.